Oxford REVISION GUIDE

GCSE

BUSINESS STUDIES
through diagrams

Andrew Gillespie

Oxford University Press

Oxford University Press, Great Clarendon Street, Oxford OX2 6DP

Oxford New York
Athens Auckland Bangkok Bogota
Buenos Aires Calcutta Cape Town Chennai Dar es Salaam
Delhi Florence Hong Kong Istanbul Karachi
Kuala Lumpur Madrid Melbourne Mexico City
Mumbai Nairobi Paris São Paulo Singapore
Taipei Tokyo Toronto Warsaw

and associated companies in
Berlin Ibadan

Oxford is a trade mark of Oxford University Press

© **Andrew Gillespie**

All rights reserved. This publication may not be reproduced, stored or transmitted, in any forms or by any means, except in accordance with the terms of licences issued by the Copyright Licensing Agency, or except for fair dealing for the purposes of research or private study, or criticism or review, as permitted under the Copyright, Designs and Patents Act 1988. Enquiries concerning reproduction outside those terms should be addressed to the Permissions Department, Oxford University Press.

First published 1998
Reprinted 1998

ISBN 0 19 832811 7 (Student's edition)
      0 19 832812 5 (Bookshop edition)

Typesetting, design and illustration by Hardlines, Charlbury, Oxford
Printed in Great Britain

CONTENTS

Revision and the exam   iv
Syllabus details   vi

AN INTRODUCTION TO BUSINESS
Organisations   1
Objectives and influences   2
Management process   3
Setting up in business   4
Types of business 1   5
Types of business 2   6
Types of business 3   7
Types of business 4   8
Small firms   9
Growth   10
The business environment   12
Money   13
Insurance   14

MARKETING
Marketing   15
Marketing research   16
Segmentation   18
Product life cycle   19
Price   20
Product   21
Distribution   23
Promotion   25
Advertising   26

FINANCE
Sources of finance   27
Accounts   28
Balance sheet   29
Depreciation   31
Profit and loss statement   32
Ratios   33
Break-even   36
Budgets, forecasts and cash flow   38

PRODUCTION
Production   40
Technology   41
Location   42
Purchasing and stocks   43

PEOPLE MANAGEMENT
Managing people   44
Recruitment and selection   45
Employment   47
Unions   49
Motivation in theory   51
Motivation in practice   52
Internal organisation of business   55

EXTERNAL FACTORS
Government   57
Types of economy   59
Legal environment   61
Economic environment   62
Unemployment   63
International trade   64
Europe   66
Social environment   68
Pressure groups   69
Change   70

INFORMATION & COMMUNICATION
Communication   71
Information technology   74
Business documents   76

THE 1990s
Success in the 1990s   77

TEST SECTION   78

Index   87

Revision and the exam

Winning requires preparation

Before the exam

The key to examination success is preparation. You need to start revising early and have a clear plan of action. Although the exams might seem like a long way off it's never too early to get started. You don't have to wait until everyone else starts - if you get ahead of the game, you will be in a strong position when the exams begin!

Organise a proper revision timetable. Write down the topics you need to study and plan when you are going to cover each one. Leave time at the end for general revision when you can bring all the topics together and focus on areas where you are still weak.

e.g Week One

    Monday Evening Business Studies (Finance)

    Tuesday Evening Geography (Weather)

    Wednesday Evening English (Shakespeare)

- Get hold of past paper questions to see how topics have been tested in the past. Your school should be able to provide you with past papers; if not, you can contact the examination board directly.

- Be active in your revision. Don't just read your notes over and over again. Test yourself on topics regularly, and practise past paper questions as much as you can.

- Make sure you get a good night's sleep before all your exams; don't try and work too late or you will be too tired to concentrate properly.

How to study

- Try to find somewhere free from distractions. It can be very difficult to work if there are lots of other people around or where it is very noisy. So try and find somewhere quiet where you will not be disturbed and where you can concentrate on your work.

- It is important to develop a proper work routine when you are revising, so that you are studying regularly for several hours every day. At the same time you do not want to work for too long on any one day. Working very late into the night will only mean that you are not fresh the next day and will not able to work effectively. Try to set aside a suitable number of hours for work each night. Work consistently but do not overwork.

- Give yourself breaks. It is very difficult for anyone to work for hours on end without a break, and it is not a very effective way of studying. Work for around half an hour at a time, then have a quick break before starting again.

- Plan your revision. You obviously have a great deal to revise in all of your subjects and so it is important to plan what needs to be covered when. Produce a revision plan early on but build in some flexibility. It is unlikely it will work exactly to plan - some topics will probably take longer than expected. Try not to concentrate only on the subjects or topics you like. If you are good at a topic already you shouldn't need to spend very long on it; put more effort into your weaker areas to improve your overall performance.

In the exam room

- Keep calm. Breathe deeply and don't panic. You will obviously be feeling worried at this stage, but so is everyone else. Remember it will all be over fairly soon, so do what you can.

- Get your timing right. Make sure you know how long the exam is and how long you intend to spend on each question. It's often a good idea to write down at the start of the exam the time when you should end one question and start another.

Don't try to work too late; get a good night's sleep before the exam

iv Revision and the exam

- Ignore other people around you. There will always be some people who can be distracting because they are shuffling their feet, coughing or dropping things. Just keep focused on your exam. Just because they have started writing, or have asked for an extra answer booklet, does not mean they are doing any better than you.

- Think before you write. Quickly check the paper to make sure the format is the one you expected. Identify any sections where you have to choose a question. Make sure you are happy about what needs to be done when and then start to read the first question, keeping your eye on the time. Only start to write when you have thought about the answer. Remember it's not the quantity but the quality of your answers which matters. Do not panic if everyone else seems to have started immediately; it does not mean they are writing good answers.

- Write clearly so the examiner can read your answers.

- Show all your workings; you can often get marks for the way in which you have calculated an answer even if the final figure is wrong.

Answering business studies exam questions

- Make sure you read the question properly. For example, 'state two advantages of a trade union to an employ*ee*' is different from 'state two advantages of a union to an employ*er*'. Always check the exact wording and make sure that you are answering the actual question which has been asked, rather than the one you wanted to be asked!

- Make sure you look at how many marks are available for a question. It is not worth spending too much time on one which is only worth two marks. Allocate your time properly so you are spending more time on the questions with more marks.

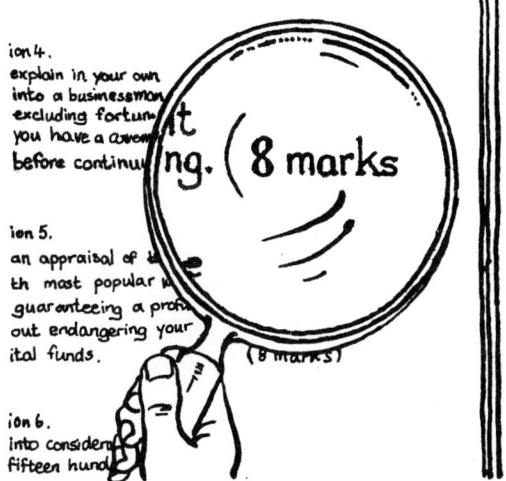

- Try to avoid spending too long on some questions simply because you know a lot about these particular topics. Remember that it's your overall mark which counts, so it is important to try every question that you are supposed to and finish the exam.

- Where possible relate your answer to the situation or business described. Think about the product, the resources, and the people involved in the given type of business. For example, a firm which has an inexperienced manager is likely to react in a different way to one with a highly skilled management team. A firm which has financial problems may not be able to afford further expansion at the moment. A firm which has a heavily branded product may not want to cut the price because it may weaken the brand.

- Where possible integrate your answers. Remember that all the departments of the business have to work together. For example, if market research suggests that there is room in the market for a new product, the firm still has to raise the finance to develop it as well as training the employees if new skills are needed and making sure it has the production capability to produce it.

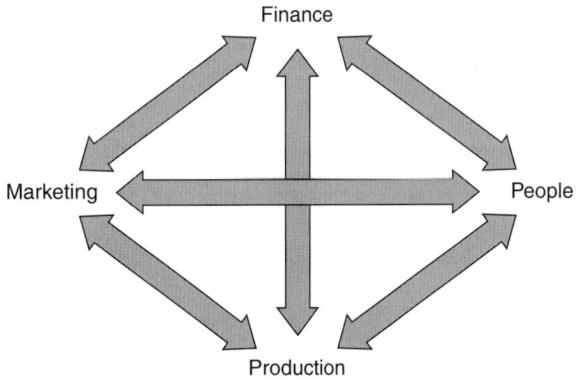

The different parts of the business are interrelated

- Check how many points you need to make. Many questions specify how many different ideas you should provide. For example, it may ask you to 'list <u>three</u> reasons', 'describe <u>two</u> types', or 'state <u>one</u> advantage'. Make sure you put down the right number. For example, if the question asks for three different ideas and carries 6 marks there will obviously be two marks per idea. If you only write one idea you can only get two marks, even if you develop it brilliantly.

Syllabus details

Assessment patterns

All GCSE Business Studies exams have a terminal (final) examination; in addition they usually have a coursework option which can carry up to 25% of the total marks. The written papers may include a pre issued case study or an unseen case study.

The overall exam tests four skills equally: demonstration of knowledge, the application of knowledge, the selection of information, and evaluation.

Assessment objectives

DEMONSTRATION OF KNOWLEDGE   25 %
e.g. do you understand what is meant by various terms, can you explain what words and concepts mean?

APPLICATION   25 %
e.g. can you apply this information to different business situations? can you use your knowledge to explain why a business might choose a particular course of action?

SELECTION   25 %
e.g. can you find relevant pieces of information? can you decide what is and what is not relevant and important?

EVALUATION   25 %
e.g. can you show judgement? can you advise a firm on the best course of action? can you justify a decision?

Tiers

Candidates will usually have a choice of two tiers:
- Foundation Tier   targeted grades   G-C
- Higher Tier   targeted grades   D-A*

Candidates failing to reach grade G on the Foundation tier or grade D on the Higher tier will be unclassified (U).
Note
All GCSE Business Studies papers assess Spelling, Punctuation, and Grammar so take care how you write your answers!

Many examination boards now offer Business Studies combined with other subjects such as Design and Technology, Information Technology, Geography or a Modern Language (French, German, and Spanish).

Midland Examining Group (MEG) Syllabus 1351

Core (Two hour written paper 50%)
Syllabus content
- External environment of the business e.g. economic environment, the business and government
- Business structure e.g. types of business organisation and raising finance
- Business behaviour e.g. marketing, production, accounts
- People in business e.g. needs and rewards and people at work
- Aiding and controlling business activity e.g. reasons for regulating business activity, influences on business activity

Optional Areas (One hour written paper 25%)
- Accounting
- Business and change
- Commerce
- Technology and change

Coursework 2500 word assignment 25%; candidates chose an assignment from a given list.

Business Studies 1352 (MEG)
Module 1 Businesses -   Coursework 25%
objectives, structure and markets

Module 2 Business management   25%
1hr 30 mins
and production
(Pre set scenario)

Module 3 and synoptic assessment   50%
2hr
The business environment
(Unseen case study - 1 hour;
2 structured questions 1 hour)

Northern Examinations and Assessment Board (NEAB) Syllabus 1411

Students have two options.
Option A
Paper 1   37.5%   (1.5 hours)
Paper 2   37.5%   (1.5 hours)
Coursework   25%

Option B
Paper 1   37.5%   (1.5 hours)
Paper 2   37.5%   (1.5 hours)
Paper 3   25%   (1 hour)

Paper 1   A case study of a simulated business situation; short answer and structured questions
Paper 2   Short answer and structured data response questions
Paper 3   A problem solving exercise based on the use of given data
Coursework   One assignment involving practical research

Subject content
1. External environment and business
2. The ownership and control of business
3. The aims and objectives of business
4. The management of people within a business
5. Finance
6. Production
7. Marketing

Southern Examining Group (SEG) Syllabus 1156

This syllabus is based on a model of 75% core plus 25% option.

Core (75%)
- The business environment
- Business structure and organisation
- Business behaviour
- People and business

Options (25%)
- Business and change
- Information technology
- Commerce
- Finance and accounting
- Enterprise

Written paper (2 hours) 75% of total marks
The written paper is based on a pre-read case study given to candidates approximately eight weeks before the examination. It will involve short answer questions and a section requiring more detailed responses.

Coursework (25%)
Candidates select one of the options i.e.

	code
Business and change	1156/3
Information technology	1156/4
Commerce	1156/5
Finance and accounting	1156/6
Enterprise	1156/7

Edexcel (BTEC/London Examinations)

Business Studies NDTEF 2400
- Subject content
- People in business - roles, relationships and management in business
- Finance - sources, uses and management of finance
- Production - production objectives and related strategies
- Marketing - marketing objectives and related strategies

Foundation Tier   Paper 1 and Coursework
Higher Tier   Paper 2 and Coursework

Paper 1 and Paper 2 (80%)
Coursework (20%) Two portfolios the first of which contains the best single unit of work from units 1 to 4 of the syllabus and the second is the research task itself.

Business Studies 1501
Subject content
- Business activity and the environment
- Structure, organisation and control of business
- Business aims and objectives
- Roles, relationships and management in business
- Sources, uses and management of finance
- Production and marketing strategies

Foundation Tier   Paper 1 and Coursework
Higher Tier   Paper 2 and Coursework

Paper 1 (2 hours):   75% short answer / multiple choice and structured questions
Paper 2 (2 hours):   75% structured / open ended questions

Coursework: 25% .One assignment which satisfies the syllabus aims. This may be chosen from a list of six prescribed assignments.

Welsh Joint Education Committee (WJEC)

Paper 1   Case Study   30%
Paper 2   (Foundation) or Paper 3 (Higher) Short answer questions and stimulus response questions   45%

Coursework   2 Assignments   25%

Northern Ireland Council for the Curriculum Examinations and Assessment

Paper 1   Pre issued Case Study   30%
Paper 2   Four compulsory multi part questions on stimulus material   50%
Coursework   20%

Get a copy of your syllabus
For more details about your syllabus, speak to your teachers or contact the examination board directly. It is always helpful to have copy of your syllabus when you are revising so you can see exactly what the examiners expect you to have covered.
Syllabuses sometimes change and so it is important to have an up to date copy.

Exam Board Addresses

Midland Examining Group (MEG)
Syndicate Buildings
1 Hills Road
Cambridge
CB1 2EU

Northern Examinations and Assessment Board (NEAB)
Devas Street
Manchester
M15 6EX

London Examinations (Edexcel)
Stewart House
32 Russell Square
London
WC1B 5DN

Southern Examining Group (SEG)
Stag Hill House,
Guildford
Surrey
GU2 5XJ

Welsh Joint Education Committee (WJEC)
245 Western Avenue
Cardiff
CF5 2YX

Northern Ireland Council for the Curriculum Examinations and Assessment (NICCEA)
Clarendon Dock
29 Clarendon Road
Belfast
BT1 3BG

Organisations

An organisation is a collection of people which exists to achieve collective goals and in which behaviour is controlled.

Organisations can be categorised by

- size — based on e.g. turnover, assets, number of employees
- sector — private sector : owned by private individuals
  public sector : owned by the Government
- activity — primary : directly related to natural resources (e.g. fishing, farming, mining)
  secondary : processing of materials e.g. manufacturing
  tertiary : services e.g. banking
- legal form — e.g. whether it is a company with a legal identity separate from its owners

---

Most of the income in the UK is increasingly generated by the tertiary sector:

% of Gross Domestic Product (at factor cost)	1964	1993
PRIMARY	5.8	3.9
SECONDARY	40.8	28.4
TERTIARY	53.8	67.7

Source : CSO

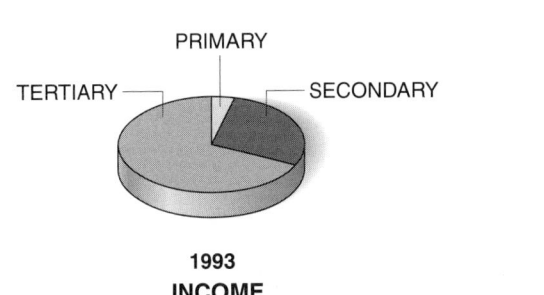

1993 INCOME

The majority of people in the UK are increasingly employed in the tertiary sector:

% of total employment	1964	1993
PRIMARY	5.1	1.5
SECONDARY	46.9	25.2
TERTIARY	47.8	73.0
Total number employed	22,357,000	21,554,000

Source : CSO, National Income and Expenditure

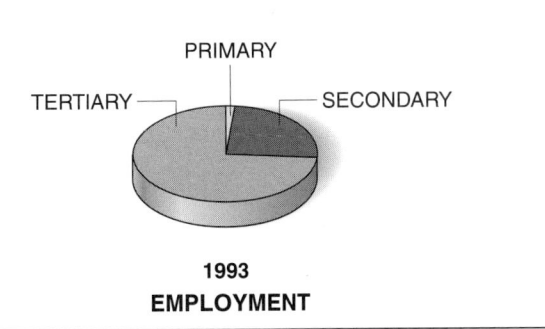

1993 EMPLOYMENT

All organisations transform inputs into outputs:

Transformation process:

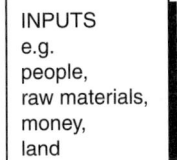

INPUTS
e.g.
people,
raw materials,
money,
land

→ TRANSFORMATION PROCESS
e.g.
extracting, manufacturing,
assembling, refining,
adding, designing,
mixing, combining

→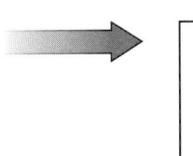

OUTPUTS
e.g.
finished
goods
and
services

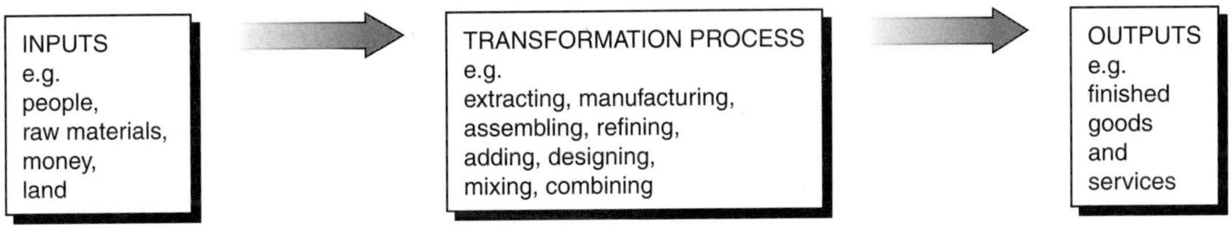

The aim of organisations is to generate outputs which have a greater value than the inputs used up. Business organisations generally value inputs and outputs in monetary terms ; therefore the aim is usually to generate a revenue which is greater than the costs i.e. to make a profit.

Competitive advantage: an aspect of the firm's behaviour or performance which gives it a competitive edge over its competitors, e.g. it may be a lower cost producer, or have a unique selling proposition (USP), such as being the only company to deliver to your door the next day.

Introduction to Business Studies 1

Objectives and influences

Objectives may include:

Survival — in the short run firms may have to sacrifice profit to survive, e.g. in a price war. Ensuring that the firm has enough cash is often a priority in the short run

Profit — profit is important to reward owners, to invest into the business and to attract investors

Growth — to gain economies of scale and to gain market power

Customer satisfaction
to increase demand and lead to long term profits

Provide a service to the public
e.g. hospitals, libraries. These organisations may not make a profit but provide a service to the community

Increase the share price
this is often important in public limited companies to make shareholders wealthier

Constraints on decision making

Internal
Factors a firm can control, but which restrict its ability to achieve its objectives.

Finance - e.g. cashflow, ability to raise finance

Marketing - e.g. limited salesforce distribution

Human resources - e.g. numbers, skills, motivation, attitudes

Production - e.g. capacity, quality, flexibility

External
Factors beyond the immediate control of the firm, which restrict its ability to achieve its objectives.

Political factors - e.g. Government policy

Economic factors - state of economy

Social factors - e.g. social trends, demographics, attitudes

Technology - e.g. rate of charge

Influences on business activity

All firms are influenced by other organisations or by individuals around them. These groups can limit a firm's behaviour and constrain their activities or help the firm to succeed.

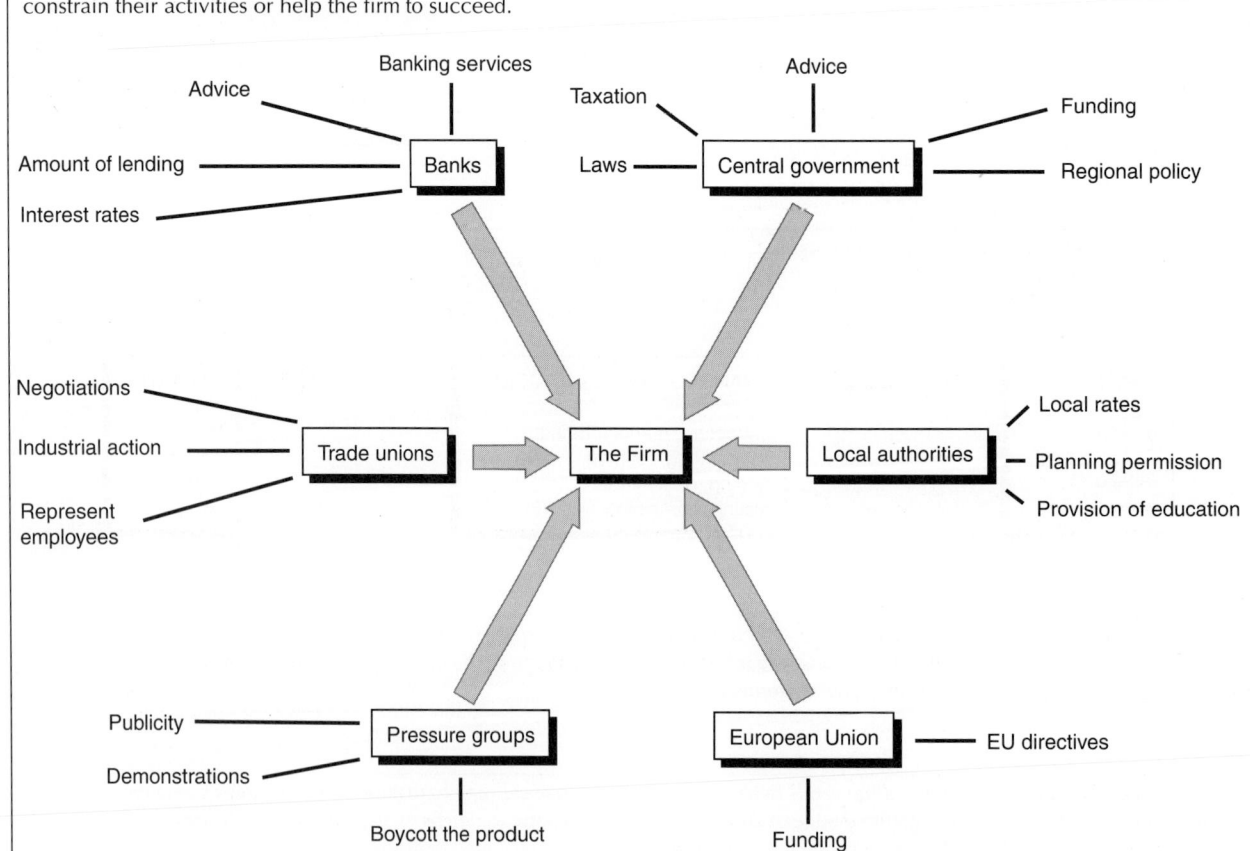

2 Introduction to Business Studies

Management process

Management is about 'getting things done through others' (R. Stewart).
It involves deciding what has to be done and how to do it; and making sure the right decisions are implemented.

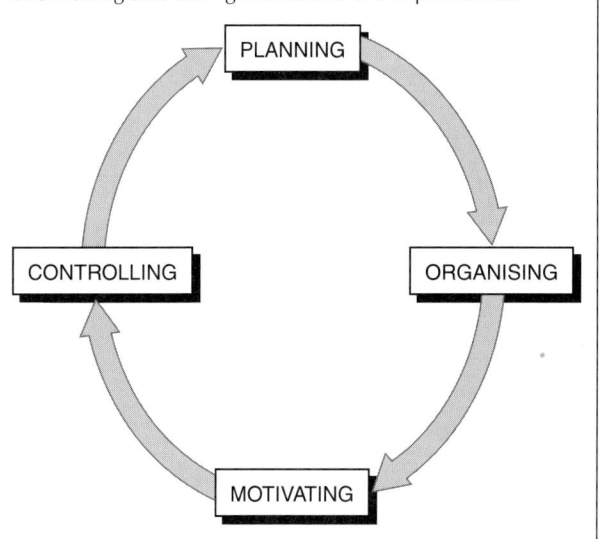

Management is a dynamic process - it is ongoing and ever changing as the challenges, resources and constraints of a firm change.

Management skills

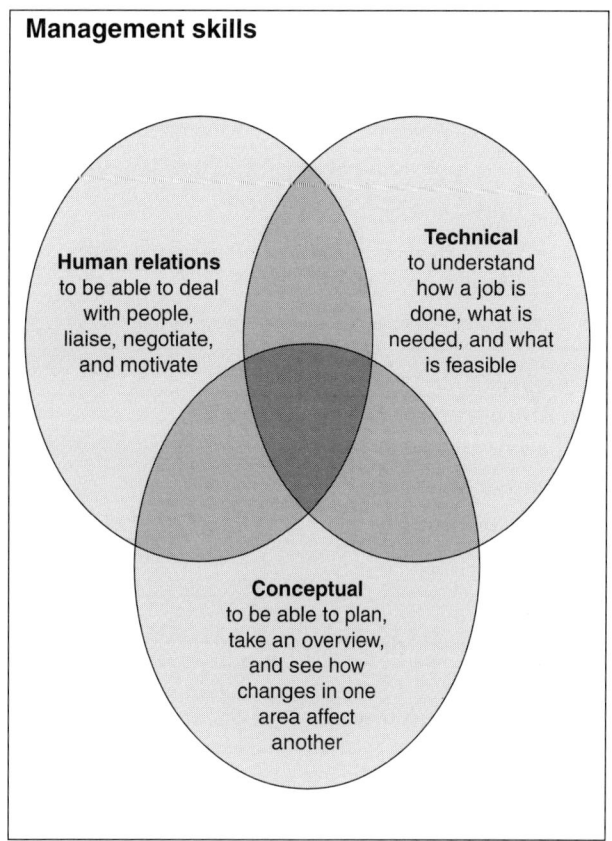

Human relations to be able to deal with people, liaise, negotiate, and motivate

Technical to understand how a job is done, what is needed, and what is feasible

Conceptual to be able to plan, take an overview, and see how changes in one area affect another

Management hierarchy

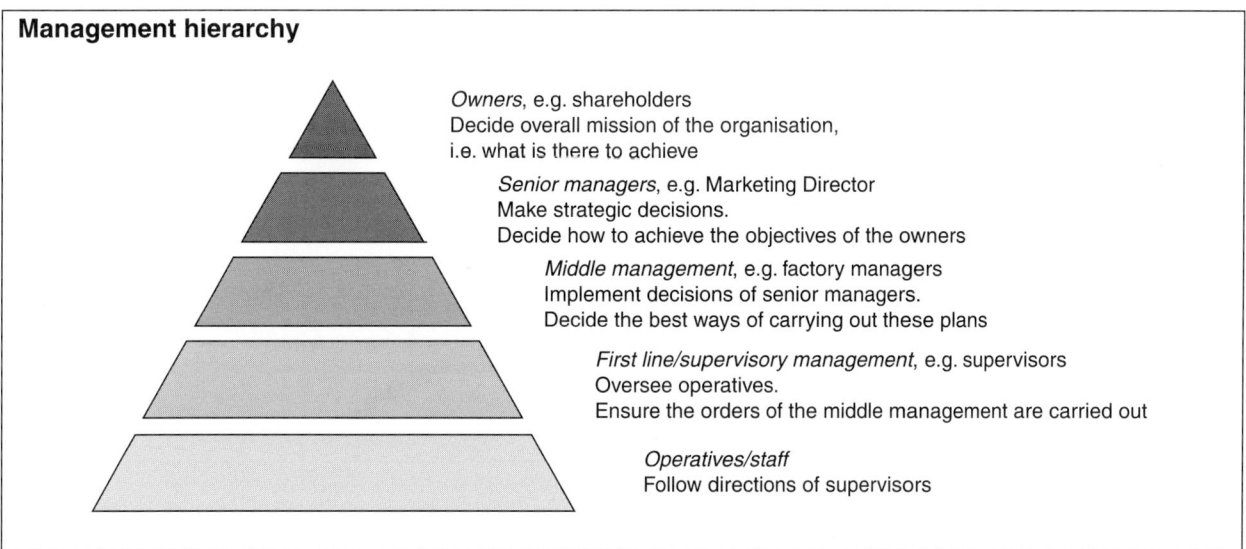

Owners, e.g. shareholders
Decide overall mission of the organisation, i.e. what is there to achieve

Senior managers, e.g. Marketing Director
Make strategic decisions.
Decide how to achieve the objectives of the owners

Middle management, e.g. factory managers
Implement decisions of senior managers.
Decide the best ways of carrying out these plans

First line/supervisory management, e.g. supervisors
Oversee operatives.
Ensure the orders of the middle management are carried out

Operatives/staff
Follow directions of supervisors

Divorce between ownership and control: the managers who control the organisation day to day may have different objectives from the owners, e.g. the managers may want to invest to grow whereas the owners may want higher dividends, i.e. there may be a divorce between their objectives.

Mission statement: states the overall aims of the organisation and its values. The aim is to develop a common sense of purpose, e.g. the mission might be 'to be the world's best airline' or 'to protect and serve'.

Objectives: must be quantifiable and time specific, e.g. to increase sales by 20% over three years.

Styles of management

Autocratic: leader tells employees

Democratic: leader discusses with employees and involves them in decisions

Laissez-faire: leader has little direct input; leaves subordinates to make decisions

Paternalistic: 'fatherly' style of leadership; employees treated as family members; leader tries to guide them; will tend to decide for them ('I know best')

Introduction to Business Studies 3

Setting up in business

People set up a business because:
- they want to work for themselves (independence)
- they have been made redundant from their last job
- they cannot find another job
- they want to achieve something for themselves (self actualisation)
- it is a natural progression from a hobby or interest

An entrepreneur is someone who:
- combines resources
- identifies opportunities
- takes risks
- makes decisions

People often set up on their own because they have a bright idea but established firms are not interested, e.g. Dyson vacuum cleaners.

To achieve the finance to set up a business, individuals often require a business plan.

Business plan: a report showing plans of the business; often used to attract finance from investors. Businesses which put time and effort into their business plans, thinking about the competition and the financial consequences of their proposals, are more likely to be successful than those which do not.

The main elements of business plan include:

- a description of the business - What does it make? What service does it provide?
- a statement of its aims - what are the aims of the business in the short and long term?
- a marketing plan - e.g. Who needs the product/service? Why? What makes it different, i.e. what is its unique selling proposition (USP)? Who is the competition? What will the price be?
- a list of key personnel - details of who is setting up the business (background, experience)

- a projected profit and loss
- a projected balance sheet
- a projected cash flow statement
- details of the finance required - What will it be used for? What is the expected rate of return for investors?

Problems setting up in business:
- raising the necessary finance
- finding a good location
- building up a reputation
- building up loyal customers

4 Introduction to Business Studies

Types of business 1

Sole trader
An individual who owns the business, e.g. a window cleaner, local shopkeeper, or hairdresser

Advantages
- can make decisions quickly
- keeps all the rewards
- easy to set up
- privacy of business affairs

Disadvantages
- limited sources of finance (e.g. own funds)
- unlimited liability, i.e. can lose personal assets
- often has limited managerial skills
- no one to share workload with
- no one to share ideas with

In 1993 there were 3.6m businesses in the UK. 2.6m of these were sole traders or partnerships without employees.

Partnership
Two or more people trading together 'carrying on business with a view to profit' (1890 Partnership Act).

A maximum of 20 partners is allowed, except for partnerships in the professions such as law and accountancy.

Advantages
- share resources/ideas
- can cover for each other, e.g. during holidays
- more sources of finance than sole trader
- partners can specialise, e.g. one may specialise in company law, another may focus on criminal law

Disadvantages
- usually unlimited liability
- limited sources of finance
- profits must be shared between partners
- slower decision making than sole trader
- decisions of one partner are binding on the others

Deed of partnership: a legal document which forms a contract between the partners. It covers issues such as the division of profits, the dissolution (closure) of the partnership; the rights of each partner; the rules for taking on new partners.

Sleeping partner: invests in partnership but does not take part in day to day business; has limited liability. At least one partner must have unlimited liability.

Co-operative
A democratic organisation where all members have one vote. It's possible to have shareholders in a co-operative, but the shareholders have one vote each rather than one vote per share. This means no one member can easily dominate.

There are several types of co-operative, e.g.

a. **Worker co-operative:** organisation owned by employees. Employees should be motivated but can have problems managing themselves.

b. **Retail co-operative** set up to benefit consumers, e.g. the CO-OP. Surpluses distributed via lower prices.

c. **Producer co-operatives:** these have a central organisation such as the Milk Marketing Board which buys and sells products for its members.

Public sector organisations
Owned or directed by the Government; no shareholders.

Examples include the BBC, the Bank of England, the armed services, and local authority services such as schools, parks, museums, and libraries. Revenue often comes from the taxpayer as well as customers. Likely to have social objectives; not just be profit oriented

Public sector organisations may be:

a. **public corporations:** these can be set up by Royal Charter e.g. BBC

b. **nationalised industries:** these are set up by Act of Parliament e.g. Post Office.

Non profit organisations, e.g. charities such as Oxfam, sports clubs, or societies; non profit objectives; often have voluntary workers.

Introduction to Business Studies 5

Types of business 2

Companies
A company has a separate legal identity from its owners. A company owns assets, and it can sue and be sued. A company is owned by shareholders. Shareholders have limited liability - i.e. they can lose the money they have invested in the business but not their personal assets.

Forming a company

memorandum of association
includes:
- name of company
- company objectives
- location of registered office
- the amount of capital a company has and the number of shares

+

articles of association
internal rules of company
e.g. rights and duties of directors, rights of shareholders, types of share, method of electing directors

sent with a Statutory Declaration (which states that the company has followed the regulations of the Companies Acts) to the Registrar of Companies who sends back a Certificate of Incorporation

Private company (Ltd)
- must have 'Ltd' after its name
- restrictions can be placed on sale of shares
- not allowed listing on stock exchange
- not allowed to advertise their shares
- usually smaller (although some are large e.g. Littlewoods)

v

Public company (Plc)
- must have PLC after its name
- can be quoted on Stock Exchange
- minimum £50,000 authorised share capital
- shareholders have right to sell their shares to whoever they want
- usually larger

All companies: must produce a set of accounts for each shareholder; a copy of the accounts is kept at Companies House. The annual report and accounts must include: a balance sheet, profit and loss, a cash flow statement, a directors' report, and an auditor's report. The annual report of a PLC is more detailed than a Ltd's.

Being quoted on the Stock Exchange
- provides access to more investors
- raises the profile of the company, and attracts more media attention

but
- the process of becoming quoted (flotation) can be expensive and time consuming
- there is no control over the sale of shares by investors - this makes the PLC vulnerable to take-over
- PLC's have to reveal more information than Ltd's

Some firms have become a PLC and then returned to being a Ltd e.g. Andrew Lloyd Webber's Really Useful Group, and Richard Branson with Virgin.

There are about 1m limited liability companies in Great Britain (excluding Northern Ireland).

'Flotation': process of becoming a PLC
To become a plc, i.e. to float, a company must:

Ltd  Plc

- produce a prospectus giving details about the company, e.g. its activities and accounts
- meet the requirements of the Company Acts and the Stock Exchange

Five largest public companies In UK:	Market Capitalisation £m April 1996
1. British Petroleum	33,434
2. Shell	29,304
3. Glaxo Welcome	27,752
4. HSBC	26,101
5. British Telecom	23,371 Source : Sunday Times 14/4/96

Shareholders elect
Directors who oversee
Managers

What is the value of a company?

Market capitalisation: market value of company; market price of shares x number of shares

Book value: value of company as stated in its accounts.

Directors : elected by shareholders; oversee managers to ensure they are working in the interests of the shareholders; the directors are the 'watchdogs' of the shareholders; the directors are responsible for the overall strategy of the company, subject to approval by the shareholders; their conditions of appointment and powers are stated in articles of association.

Non executive directors are - part timers who have no day to day involvement (no executive powers) in the organisation

Company Secretary : company official with responsibility for maintaining a register of shareholders, notifying shareholders of annual general meeting, and preparing the company's annual returns.

6 Introduction to Business Studies

Types of business 3

Different types of shares

Ordinary shareholders
- have one vote per share
- can attend annual general meeting (AGM)
- are sent company accounts
- receive a dividend if one is paid
- can vote on directors

Preference shares
- have no vote
- receive a fixed dividend
- are paid in preference to ordinary shares but after loan repayments

Types of share capital

Authorised: maximum value of shares which company can issue; listed in the articles of association.

Issued: amount of shares actually issued. The issued share capital cannot be greater than the authorised.

Called up share capital: face value of all the shares paid for by shareholders.

Types of share issue

- **public issue:** shares are sold directly to the public
- **offer for sale:** shares are sold to an issuing house which sells them on to the public
- **placing:** shares are sold in large quantities to the institutions
- **rights issue:** shares are sold to existing shareholders.

Owning other companies

Holding company: controls other companies but is not involved in their day to day running.

Subsidiary: B is a subsidiary of A if A has more than 50% of the shares in B or has a controlling interest.

Associate company: B is an associate company of A if A has between 20 and 50% of the shares of B.

Stock exchange: market for shares; mainly second hand shares are traded i.e. shares which have already been issued by companies. In 1993 there were 1,927 UK and Irish companies with a full listing on the London Stock Exchange.

FTSE- Financial Times Stock Exchange - an index of the share prices of the top 100 companies listed in the Financial Times. Its base is 1000.

Share price

The price of a share is determined by:
- the number of issued shares
- the expected dividends
- stockbrokers' and analysts' reports
- the rates of return available elsewhere
- the present and expected profitability of the company

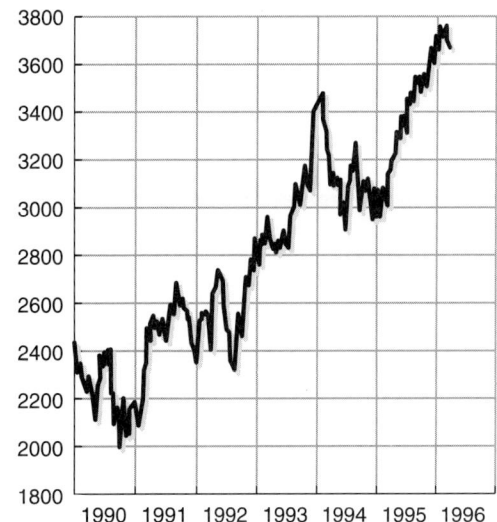

FTSE 100 - PRICE INDEX

Ownership of shares in the UK

The main shareholders in the UK are financial institutions, such as pension funds, not individuals.

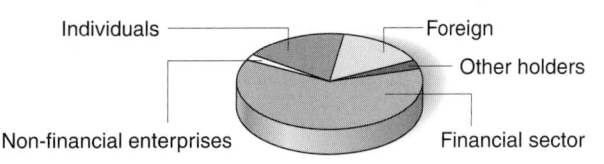

Introduction to Business Studies 7

Types of business 4

Franchises
A franchisor sells the right to use/sell a product or service to a franchisee in return for a fixed fee and/or percentage of the turnover, for example: McDonald's, Unigate Dairies, Hertz, Kall Kwik

Why buy a franchise?
- existing, established product; already known, therefore, cheaper market research and promotional costs
- may receive help and training from franchisor
- can share marketing costs, research findings, new product development costs
- lower start up costs

Why sell a franchise?
- quicker growth; can cover a geographic area more quickly
- provides funds
- managers more motivated as they own the franchise

Management buy outs
Existing managers take over the company, e.g. Oxford Bus Company. Often companies are sold to managers when an organisation is 'unbundling' (i.e. getting back to its core business), or when a business is privatised.

Multinationals:
Firms with production bases in more than one country; they may have locations around the world but have their headquarters in one country, e.g. BP, Shell, Ford

Reasons for becoming multinational:
- to make use of resources abroad e.g. raw materials
- to be closer to markets
- to avoid legislation in their own country which may prevent firms getting too big
- to gain tax advantages or grants from overseas governments
- weakens domestic unions by spreading bases around the world

Why should a government welcome a multinational?
- provides jobs
- pays taxes
- provides skills and management techniques
- provides goods and services
- reduces levels of imports

Why should a government be suspicious?
- may not share skills or knowledge
- may not invest in country
- may not train locals
- may pressurise government

Reaction should depend on which multinational it is and the extent to which it will be or can be regulated.

Joint ventures/ strategic alliances
Companies work together on specific projects. They can share costs and profits, e.g. Ford and Mazda produce cars together.

Closure of a business
1986 Insolvency Act: covers the options open to a company which is insolvent. An insolvent company may seek a voluntary agreement under which company and creditors agree to a scheme of reduced or delayed payments.

If this is not possible, a firm may ask for a bankruptcy court to appoint an 'administrator' to try to reorganise the company. If successful, the administrator returns the company to its management. If unsuccessful, the next stage is receivership - assets are sold to pay off secured creditors. If the company still cannot be saved, it may be 'wound up' - assets sold and proceeds distributed amongst its creditors.

If an individual is insolvent this is called 'bankruptcy'.

Why do firms fail?
- poor planning
- cashflow problems
- overtrading
- increased competition
- decline of market
- failure to react to market trends

Small firms

Small firms

The definition of a "small" firm varies. In the UK the Department of Trade has the following definitions:

- 'micro' - up to nine people
- 'small' - ten to ninety-nine people
- 'medium' - one hundred to four hundred and ninety-nine people

Other official definitions of small use a turnover of less than £1m or £500,000 as well as fewer than 200 or 500 employees.

The 1971 Bolton Committee concluded small firms had three main characteristics:

- relatively small share of the market
- managed by owners and part owners in a personalised way without a formal management structure
- not part of a larger organisation (e.g. not owned by another larger company)

Statistics on small firms

- small and medium-sized businesses account for about two thirds of private sector employment
- small companies account for nearly one quarter of gross domestic product
- 97% of UK businesses have a turnover of less than £1m
- 78% of UK business have a turnover of less than £100,000

How do small firms survive?

- they offer a personal service
- they serve niche markets
- they have greater flexibility
- they are innovative

Why do governments like small firms?

- they are innovative
- they create jobs
- they fill niches
- they provide competition for larger firms
- they sell abroad increasing exports

Government help

- Alternative Investment Market - provides market for shares of smaller firms without as many regulations and expenses as a full listing on the Stock Exchange. (replaces Unlisted Securities Market USM)
- Loan Guarantee Scheme - government guarantees a proportion of a small firm's loan in return for a fee. Provides small firms with more opportunity to borrow.
- Information and advice - e.g. Training and Enterprise Councils.
- Business Start Up Scheme - provides financial help for unemployed individuals setting up new businesses (previously the Enterprise Allowance).
- Tax allowances - small firms pay a reduced rate of corporation tax.
- Enterprise Investment Scheme - Income tax relief for investors in small companies (previously the Business Expansion Scheme).
- Enterprise Initiative grants for small companies employing less than 25 people in development areas.
- Small Firms Merit Award for Research and Technology (SMART) - financial support for development of new technology with commercial potential for firms with less than 50 employees.
- Support for Products Under Research (SPUR) - funds for development of new products and processes for firms with less than 250 employees.
- Less government interference - in the 1980s and 1990s various schemes have been introduced to reduce government regulations and bureaucracy for small firms, e.g. the accounts small companies have to file are simpler than for larger companies.

Sources of advice for small firms include:

- Training and enterprise Councils (TECs)
- Local Chambers of Commerce
- Local Enterprise Agencies (LEAs)
- Business Links (brings together the services of, e.g. TECs, LEAs, and Chambers of Commerce in one location)

Growth

Size

The size of a firm can be measured in a number of ways, e.g. assets, employees, turnover.

A firm may be large using one indicator but small using another, e.g. the National Health Service has a large number of employees but a low turnover.

Types of Growth

Internal
- Firm expands without involving other businesses.
- 'Organic' growth involves expanding by selling more of existing products.
- Often slower.

External
- Can be via aquisition/take-over or merger.
- Quicker.

Integration

Integration occurs when two or more firms join together - it might be through a merger or a take-over

Merger: mutual agreement between two or more companies to join together.

Why merge?
- Share resources
- Gain economies of scale
- Quick growth

Problems merging
- Clash of management styles
- Government may prevent it if it forms a monopoly

Takeover: occurs when one firm gains control of another. It may be via a cash offer or a paper offer (offer shares in own company in return for shares in target company) or a combination of the two.

10 Introduction to Business Studies

Types of integration

Type of integration	Description	Possible reasons
Horizontal	same stage of same production process	market power, economies of scale
Vertical	different stage of same production process	control suppliers or outlets
Conglomerate	different production process	spread risks

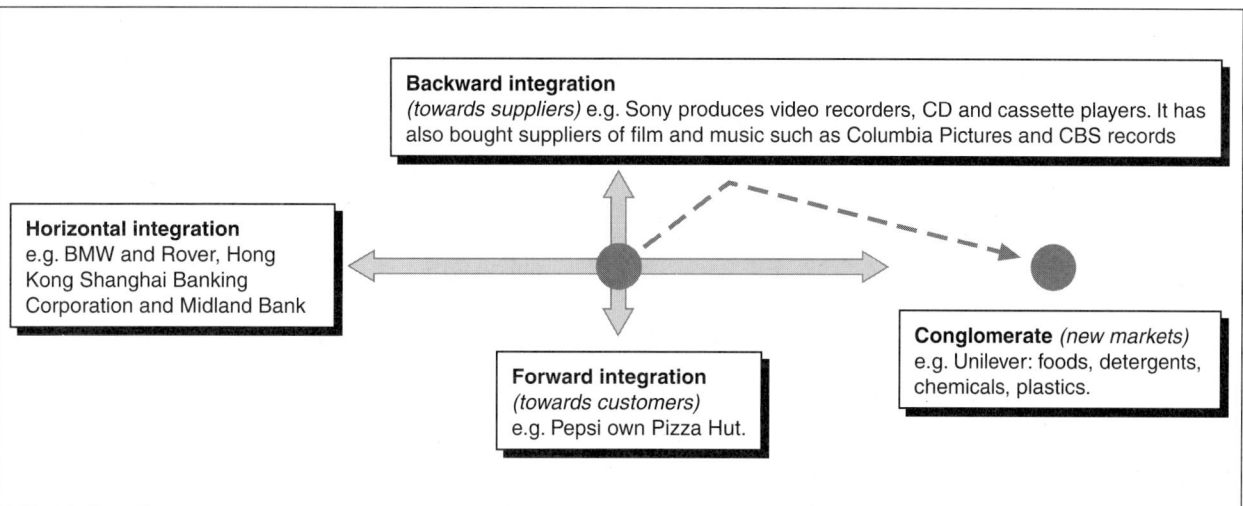

Backward integration
(towards suppliers) e.g. Sony produces video recorders, CD and cassette players. It has also bought suppliers of film and music such as Columbia Pictures and CBS records

Horizontal integration
e.g. BMW and Rover, Hong Kong Shanghai Banking Corporation and Midland Bank

Conglomerate *(new markets)*
e.g. Unilever: foods, detergents, chemicals, plastics.

Forward integration
(towards customers)
e.g. Pepsi own Pizza Hut.

Internal economies of scale

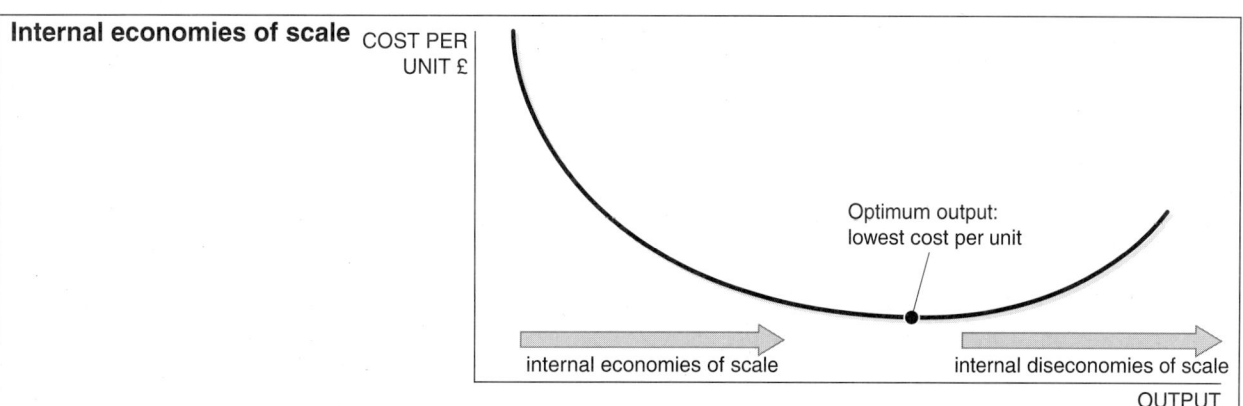

Internal economies of scale
Cost advantage of producing on a larger scale. As output increases, cost per unit falls.

- Financial - cheaper borrowing as firm gets bigger and has more assets and collateral
- Managerial - can employ specialists, number of managers will not grow at same rate as sales
- Technical - can use mass production techniques; division of labour (employees, specialise)
- Purchasing - discounts for bulk buying, can negotiate better terms
- Risk bearing economies - less risk as can diversify into different areas.

Diseconomies of scale
If firm gets too big the costs per unit may increase. This is due to problems with:

- communicating
- co-ordinating
- controlling
- motivating as individuals get 'lost in the crowd'.

External economies of scale
These are cost savings which can help a firm become more competitive. Internal economies occur because the firm increases its output; external economies occur because of factors outside the firm.

- economies of disintegration - When an industry grows some firms might specialise in particular parts of the process. This can lead to higher quality and cheaper supplies and services for all the firms in the industry.
- economies of concentration - These occur when many firms in an industry locate in a particular area. Because the industry is based in one area, specialist facilities usually develop e.g. local training colleges, specialist export and financial advice. Firms will also benefit from sharing knowledge and being in close contact with each other.

The business environment

Organisations are continually reacting to changes in the environments in which they operate. To make effective decisions organisations must constantly scan their environment to identify change and prepare for it.

- **Macroenvironment:** factors beyond the immediate control of the firm

  PEST factors, Political, Economic, Social, Technological; can also be categorised as SLEEPT: social, legal, economic, environmental, political, and technological factors

- **Microenvironment:** factors in the immediate environment of the firm,

  e.g. Suppliers, Workforce, Investors, Customers, Distributors. Organisations can influence micro factors more easily than macro factors.

- **Internal environment:** the functions of the organisation e.g. marketing, production, finance, and personnel

Stakeholders: stakeholders are groups with a 'stake' or interest in the organisation, e.g. customers, employees, the government, shareholders. Organisations increasingly believe that success comes through co-operating with stakeholder groups.

Conflicting interests: e.g. employees may want more pay but in the short term this may have to come out of shareholders' rewards; government may want firms to hold their prices and not contribute to inflation, but owners may want a price increase to cover higher costs.

Markets: A firm's behaviour will be influenced by the type of market it operates in.

- Monopoly - in theory a single producer; in reality it occurs when one firm dominates a market; the Monopolies and Mergers Commission define a monopoly as a firm which has more than 25% of the market.
- Oligopoly - several firms dominate the market, e.g. petrol, cigarettes, and washing powders. Cartel - firms acting together (colluding) to control price and output, e.g OPEC (Oil Petroleum and Exporting Countries).
- Perfect competition - many firms producing

  Concentration ratio measures the extent to which a market is controlled by a given number of firms. Usually measures their percentage of total market sales, e.g. a 4 firm concentration ratio of 80% means that the largest four firms have 80% of the markets' sales.

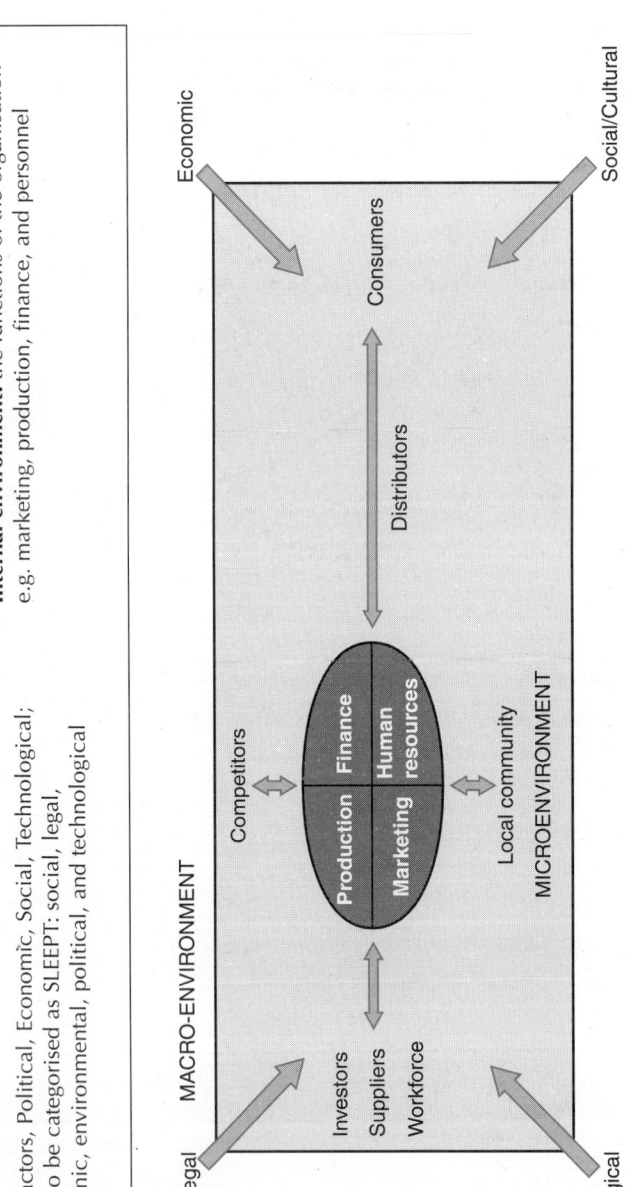

Functions

Marketing: concerned with, e.g. identifying market opportunities, developing new products, distributing them, promoting and selling them.

Production: concerned with, e.g. research and development, production methods, stock control, quality control, and production levels.

Finance: concerned with, e.g. raising finance, measuring and controlling financial inflows and outflows, maintaining financial records, financial planning.

Personnel Management concerned with, e.g. identifying human resource requirements, the recruitment and selection of employees, training, developing, assessing, promoting and transferring people

These functions are interrelated. For example, an increase in sales may require more employees (human resource management), more production, modifications to products (production function), or a new advertising campaign (marketing) and funds for initial promotional expenditure (finance)

12 Introduction to Business Studies

Money

Uses
- **medium of exchange:** it can be used in exchange for goods and services
- **unit of account:** it can be used to measure the value of goods and services
- **store of value:** it usually keeps its value over time so people are willing to hold on to it

Features of money
Money has to be
- acceptable i.e. people must be willing to accept it as payment
- durable: it has to last a long time
- portable: people must be able to carry it around
- scarce: there must be a limited amount of it so that it has a value

Credit cards
Individuals can spend up to their credit limit; the amount they spend is paid back in regular instalments

Charge cards
The amount which is borrowed must be paid off in total each month e.g. American Express

Debit cards
These are used to take money directly out of a person's bank account. No credit is involved e.g. Switch and Delta

Types of bank account
- cheque accounts - these do not usually pay much interest but money can be taken out at any time. Also called 'current accounts'.
- deposit accounts - these pay interest but you may have to give notice before any money can be taken out.
- foreign currency accounts - these allow firms to keep their money in the form of foreign currency. This is useful for businesses which trade abroad a great deal.
- money market accounts - these are normally only used by large companies. They are for large sums of money which are then borrowed for very short periods of time by other institutions including the government.

Banking services
Banks such as Barclays and Lloyds lend money to firms. They also provide a range of other services including:
- standing orders - used to arrange for a specific amount of money to be paid out of your account on particular days e.g. a certain amount might be paid every month to pay for insurance.
- direct debits - with a direct debit money can be taken directly out of your bank account e.g. you might pay your telephone bill on direct debit. Unlike a standing order the amount taken out will vary according to how big your bill is.
- a banker's draft - a banker's draft guarantees payment. A cheque may bounce (i.e. be returned if there is not enough money in the account) or be stopped (when the person who wrote the cheque instructs the bank not to pay it). Neither of these can happen with a draft.
- safeguarding valuables - banks will look after important valuables for customers; businesses which are largely paid in cash can use their night safes (these are safes built into the outside wall of a bank)
- provide advice e.g. to people setting up a business
- provide help with international payments e.g. arrange bills of exchange or letters of credit

Savings

The best place to save depends on:
- the amount of money you want to save
- how quickly you may need to get at it. The longer you are prepared to leave your money in a bank or building society the better the rate of interest. This is because the banks and building societies have more time to use the money for themselves.
- how much risk you are willing to take, e.g. investing in shares is riskier than investing in a building society because the share price may go down as well as up. However, if the shares do increase in value the overall return may be higher.

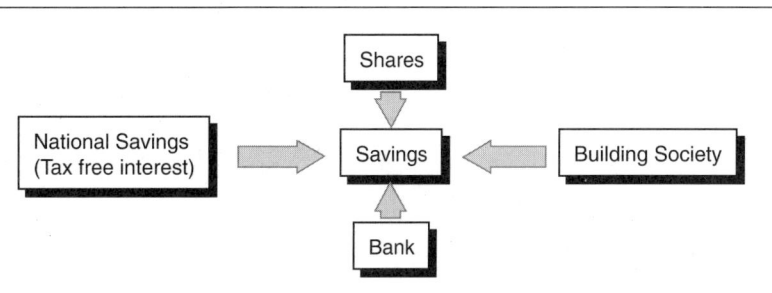

Introduction to Business Studies 13

Insurance

Insurance: helps to reduce risk. By taking out buildings and contents insurance, for example, firms will receive a payment if there is a fire or flood.

'cover': insurance cover means that the person has protection if a particular event occurs e.g. if you have fire cover this means you will receive money if your factory burns down.

Pooling the risk: individuals cannot usually afford to keep enough money to cover the possibility of an accident happening. As a result people started to 'pool their risk' by all paying a certain amount of money every month into a 'pool' or fund which can be used to pay out if one of the members does actually have an accident. This is how the insurance market began.

Insurance companies work out the risk of an accident happening and individuals and businesses pay into the scheme to cover the possibility of risk of an accident.

The amount paid into the insurance scheme is called the **'insurance premium'**.

Insurance policy: the document setting out the precise terms on which insurance cover has been provided.

Uninsurable risks: these are risks which the firms cannot insure against e.g. a badly designed product, competitors launching a better product. Insurance companies cannot calculate the risk of these events and so cannot offer insurance.

Insurance and assurance

Insurance provides cover for something which might happen, e.g. an accident

Assurance provides cover for something which will definitely happen some time, e.g. you put money into a life assurance scheme which pays out when you die.

Types of insurance

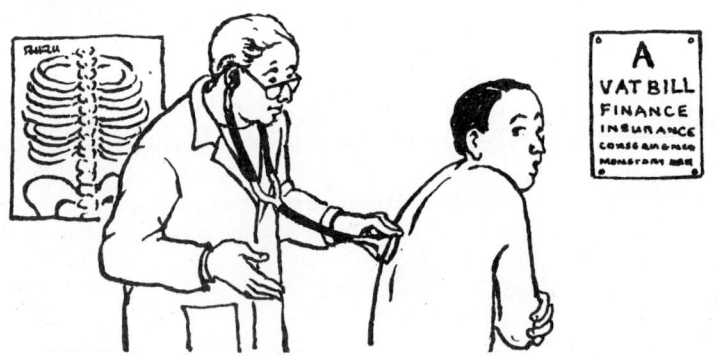

- health insurance to pay for hospital treatment
- employers' liability - covers accidents or illnesses that happen as a result of employees' work
- product liability - covers accidents or injuries as a result of using the product
- key man cover - this is taken out to cover the risk of death of a senior figure e.g. the managing director
- buildings and contents - to cover the direct effects of an accident or disaster e.g. a fire or a flood
- consequential loss - this covers the indirect effects of an accident e.g. the time it takes to find new premises, the loss of goodwill, the loss of custom.
- fidelity insurance to cover theft and fraud by staff
- public liability insurance - this covers any accident which might happen to the general public e.g. when they are visiting a company's premises. All companies must have this insurance by law.
- motor vehicle insurance - covers damage to any of the firm's motor vehicles
- bad debts insurance - covers the risk of customers not paying for the goods
- goods in transit insurance - covers goods whilst they are being moved around.

Insurance people

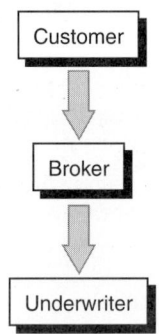

- broker - the broker deals directly with the customer and finds the most appropriate underwriter to carry the risk. Most of the larger brokers are members of Lloyds.
- underwriters - these are the companies which accept the risk. Cover for very high risk may be carried by several underwriters.
- assessors - assess the extent of the damage and decide how much a person is entitled to receive.
- actuaries - calculate the extent of the risk for insurance companies so that they can decide what to charge the customer.

Lloyds (of London)

A corporation made up of many insurance brokers and insurance companies. Lloyds itself does not do any underwriting but its members arrange insurance cover either individually or acting as a group (forming a syndicate).

Marketing

Marketing: identifying, anticipating and meeting customer needs and wants in a mutually beneficial process. It must be beneficial for both sides; it involves meeting the organisation's objectives as well as the customers'.

Market and product orientation

Market orientation: The organisation focuses on customer needs and wants. The starting point of its planning is what customers want.

CUSTOMER ⟶ ORGANISATION

'The purpose of a business is to get and keep a customer'.
Theodore Levitt

Product orientation: The organisation focuses on what it wants to do and hopes customers will buy.

ORGANISATION ⟶ CUSTOMER

Product orientation can be successful if there is limited competition (e.g. a monopoly or protected market), but nowadays firms generally need to be more market oriented. For example, in the 1980s British Airways paid too much attention to their planes and not enough to their customers; they were too product oriented.

Why is market orientation becoming more important?
Greater competition, shorter life-cycles, consumers more demanding, markets more fragmented, competitors have a clearer idea of customer needs, customers are more informed and choice is easier, markets are more open.

Marketing mix: the tools of marketing.

The best known elements of the marketing mix are the four P's:

- Price
  e.g. What does it cost the consumer? Are there easy payment terms? Are there discounts?

- Product
  e.g. What does it do? What does it look like?

- Promotion
  e.g. How does the consumer find out about it? What are they told?

- Distribution (Place)
  e.g. How does it get to the consumer? Direct from the manufacturer or via intermediaries?

However, it is possible to include others:

- People   What are the staff like? Are they well trained? Cooperative?

- Process   Is the buying process easy, e.g. can customers pay by credit card? How many forms are there to fill in? Can the goods be bought by phone?

Marketing mix

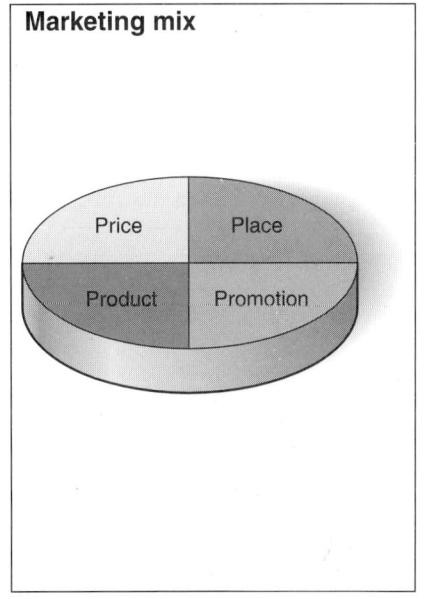

Niche market - a small part of the market which major producers are not concerned with, e.g Privilege offers car insurance for high risk categories such as high performance cars and young drivers.

Mass market - market with a large volume or value of sales, e.g. soap powders.

Dangers of niche marketing:
- large producers may enter the market if it proves successful
- the firm may be too reliant on one product so high risk
- the firm will not benefit from economies of scale

Markets

Market size - value of sales in the market; measured by number of units sold or value of sales.

Market share - a firm or product's market share is its percentage of all the sales in the market. It can be measured as a percentage of the number of units sold or of the value of sales, e.g. if market sales are £50,000 and a firm's sales are £10,000 then the firm has a 20% market share.

An example of market shares

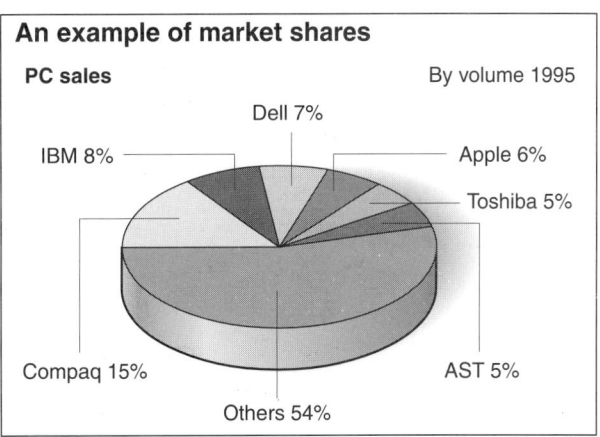

PC sales — By volume 1995
IBM 8%, Dell 7%, Apple 6%, Toshiba 5%, AST 5%, Others 54%, Compaq 15%

Marketing 15

Marketing research

Marketing research: Gathering, recording, analysing, and presenting information relevant to the marketing process. Marketing research provides information to help firms make better decisions

Marketing research gathers and analyses information to help the firm's marketing

Research is used to:
- identify opportunities and threats, e.g. How is the market changing?
- analyse alternative courses of action, e.g. Would a price change be more effective than more advertising?
- review progress, e.g. monitor sales after a promotional campaign

When undertaking research a firm will:
- identify a problem
- decide a method of gathering data, e.g. field or desk research; postal survey or face to face
- gather the data
- analyse the data
- present its findings

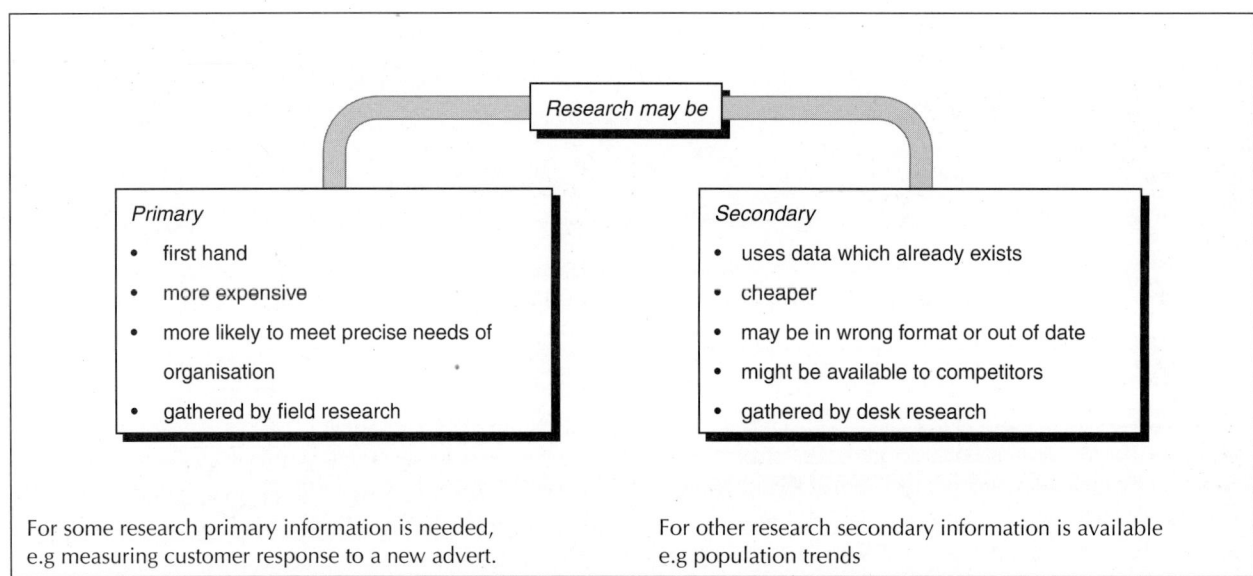

Research may be

Primary
- first hand
- more expensive
- more likely to meet precise needs of organisation
- gathered by field research

Secondary
- uses data which already exists
- cheaper
- may be in wrong format or out of date
- might be available to competitors
- gathered by desk research

For some research primary information is needed, e.g measuring customer response to a new advert.

For other research secondary information is available e.g population trends

Qualitative research: is research into peoples' motivation, feelings, behaviour. It may be undertaken in discussion groups or individual interviews

Sources of secondary data:
- Internal data - e.g. sales records, production records
- Government: e.g. Social Trends, Census, Annual Abstract of Statistics, Monthly Digest of Statistics (data on, e.g. output and balance of payments), Bank of England Quarterly Bulletin, Blue Book (national income)
- Independent Forecasting Groups e.g. Henley Centre
- Newspapers e.g. Financial Times
- Trade associations and trade magazines e.g. Campaign (for the advertising industry)

Marketing research continued

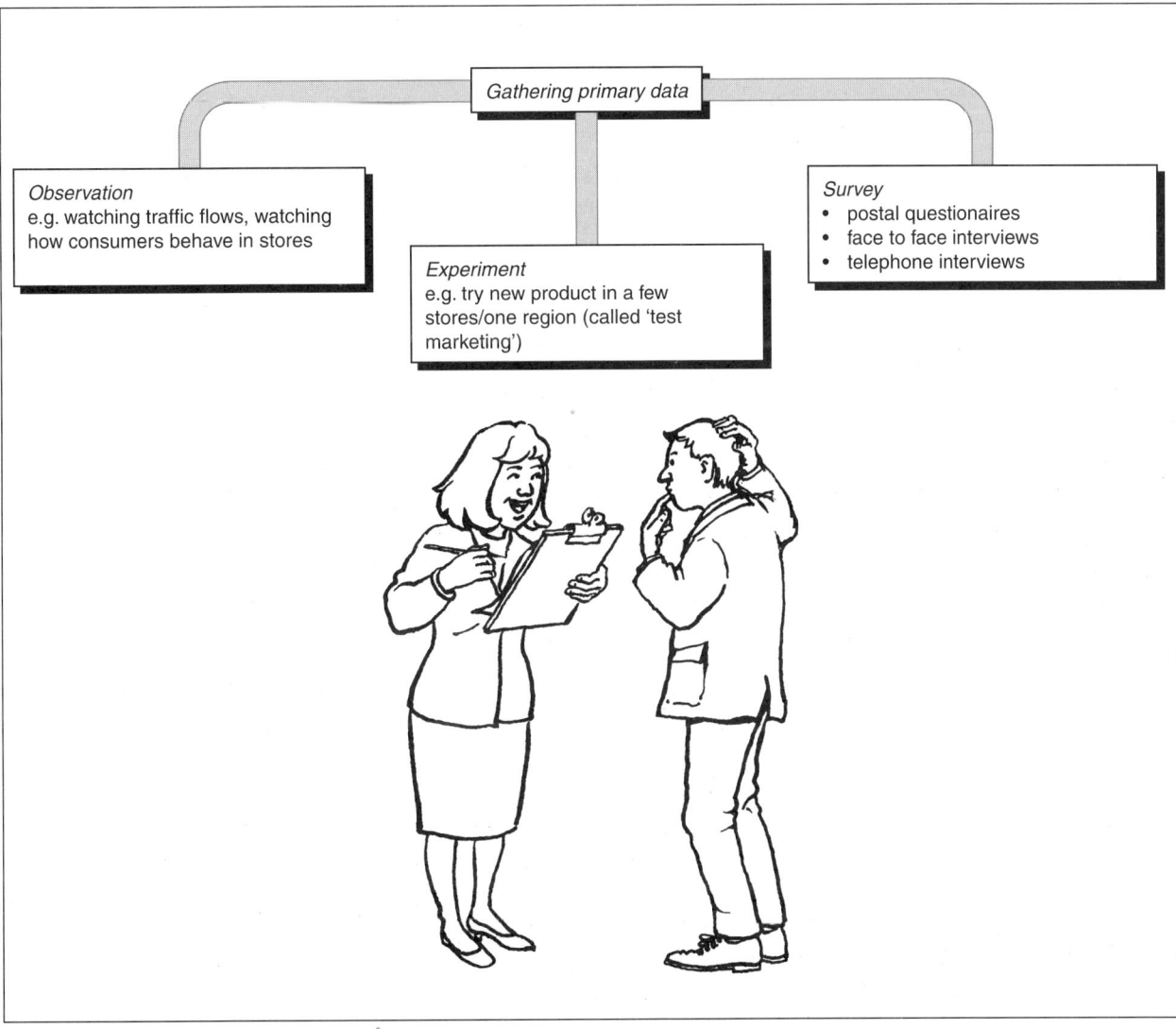

Internal v external data

Internal data is information gathered within the firm itself, e.g. from its own sales records.

External data is information gathered from outside of the firm, e.g. from customers, from competitors, from market research agencies.

Samples:

Population - the total number of items or people the researcher is interested in.

Census - a survey of the total population. Not usually feasible due to time and expense.

To save time and money, researchers may take a **sample**. This is a small group which is thought to represent the market as a whole.

Deciding on the best method of research

- How much will it cost?
- How long will it take?
- What alternatives are there?
- How important is it that we know?
- What is the risk if we do not do research?
- How reliable will the findings be (i.e. if the research was repeated would the firm get the same results)?

Research does not guarantee success but can help to reduce the risk.

Not all research uses formal researching methods. Some decisions are based on intuition or hunch.

Marketing 17

Segmentation

Segmentation: identifying groups of relatively similar needs and wants within a market. The firm can then develop an appropriate marketing mix for each segment. The aim is to meet customer needs more precisely. The problem is that it may cost more to develop new versions of a product or service.

Methods of segmentation:

- Age — e.g. magazines for different age groups (e.g. Just 17), adult snacks (e.g Phileas Fogg), Landmark Express offer cheaper car insurance for people over 45, Club 18-30 holidays obviously target a particular age-group.

- Gender — e.g. certain cars are targeted at women drivers some toys are aimed more at boys (e.g. Action Man), others target girls (e.g. Barbie).

- Socio-Economic groups — e.g. newspapers target different Socio-Economic groups.

e.g.
A	upper middle class	higher managerial/professional e.g lawyer
B	middle class	middle managerial/administrative/professional e.g manager
C1	lower middle class	supervisors, clerks, junior managers e.g shop assistant
C2	skilled working class	skilled manual worker e.g mechanic
D	working class	semi skilled/unskilled manual e.g cleaner
E	subsistence level	unemployed or state pensioner

- Location — e.g. board games sell better in colder climates; outdoor games are more popular in warmer regions

- An individual's stage in the life cycle — e.g the housing market consists of first time buyers, people trading up and retirement buyers; magazines – *Practical Parenting*

- Family size — e.g family packs of food, design of houses

- Usage rates — e.g frequent wash shampoo

- Lifestyle — e.g convenient, microwaveable food for young, single, working people

- Benefit — e.g people buy toothpaste for different benefits, including the taste, fresh breath and to keep their teeth white

- Psychographical (motives for buying) — e.g. reasons why people buy chocolates include to reward themselves, to relax, to share, to give to others.

Segmentation: Different products may be made for different segments of the market

18 Marketing

Product life cycle

Product life cycle: shows stages in a product's life. It is a model used to aid decision making.

The shape and length of the life cycle will differ from one product to another. Some life cycles last years (e.g. Kellogg's Cornflakes); others are more short-lived (e.g. Teenage Mutant Ninja Turtles.)

Stages of the life cycle: development, introduction, growth, maturity, decline

	Development	Intro-duction	Growth	Maturity	Decline
		electric cars video 'phones	CD ROMs fax machines	colour tv's washing machines	black & white tv s typewriters

Development Product is being developed and tested. This may take years, e.g. a new car or new film or may take hours, e.g. a new recipe in a restaurant. Losses are often made due to heavy development costs.

Introduction Sales often slow. Distributors may be reluctant to take a new unproved product. Heavy promotion to make consumers aware. High level of risk. High unit production costs; no economies of scale.

Growth Sales begin to grow rapidly. Competition beginning to enter the market. Cost per unit falling; economies of scale. Profits usually made.

Maturity Sales growth is slower. More competition. Promotion stresses differences with competition. The firm will try to develop/maintain brand loyalty.

Decline Sales declining. Profits falling. Substitutes appear.

Examples of life cycles

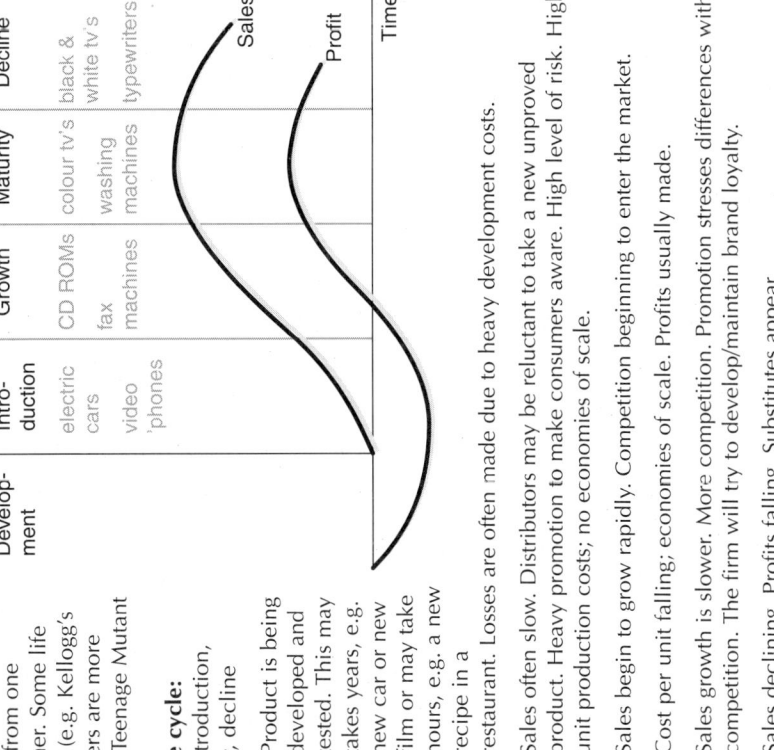

A 'fad' product, e.g. Rubik's cube, Buzz Lightyear toys

New uses found for product, e.g. 'Kevlar' is a material used for bullet proof vests, skis, boats, helmets

Product is revived, e.g. Lucozade, Star Wars, Flared trousers, Ovaltine

Value of life cycle:

highlights different stages in a typical life cycle and the need to adjust marketing strategies and tactics at each stage. However, it is only a model. The decision maker must take account of different markets and different ways in which products may develop. There is a danger of it become self-fulfilling, e.g because firms expect a decline in sales they fail to devote enough resources to a product to enable sales to be maintained.

Extension strategies: attempt to prolong the maturity stage and stop sales declining. A firm may:

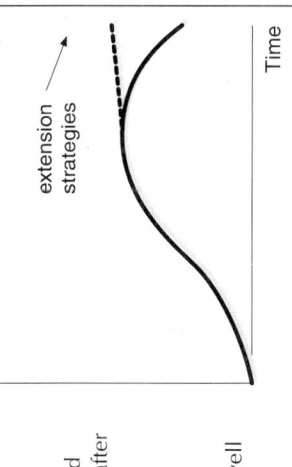

- Modify the product, e.g. 'new' 'added' 'extra' ingredients
- Promote more heavily, e.g. more advertising
- Develop complimentary products, e.g. extend the product range - add shaving cream and after shave to shampoo and conditioner products
- Find new uses for the product
- Attempt to increase usage, e.g. encourage customers to eat cereals in the evenings as well as the mornings

Marketing 19

Price

Element of the marketing mix

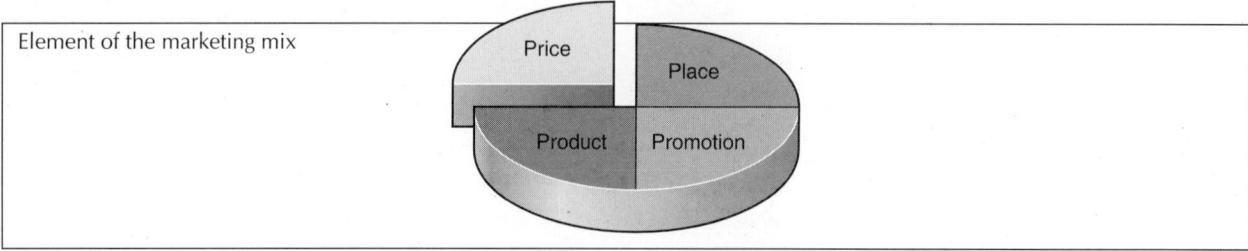

The price of a good or service may depend on:

- costs - organisations will generally want to cover their costs to make a profit for investment and to reward their owners
- demand - i.e. What is the level of demand and how sensitive is demand to price?
- competition - i.e How similar are their products? What price are they charging?
- government - e.g. the Government places indirect taxes (such as VAT) on most goods, which increases costs
- objectives - e.g. short term or long term profits
- stage of the life cycle, e.g. the price is more likely to increase in the growth phase and fall in decline
- rest of the mix, e.g. Is it positioned as a more exclusive item than competitors; products?

The price is likely to be higher when:

- the good is heavily branded
- the good is distributed to exclusive outlets
- it is a speciality good
- the good is at the growth stage of the life cycle
- the firm is following a skimming strategy

Methods of pricing include:

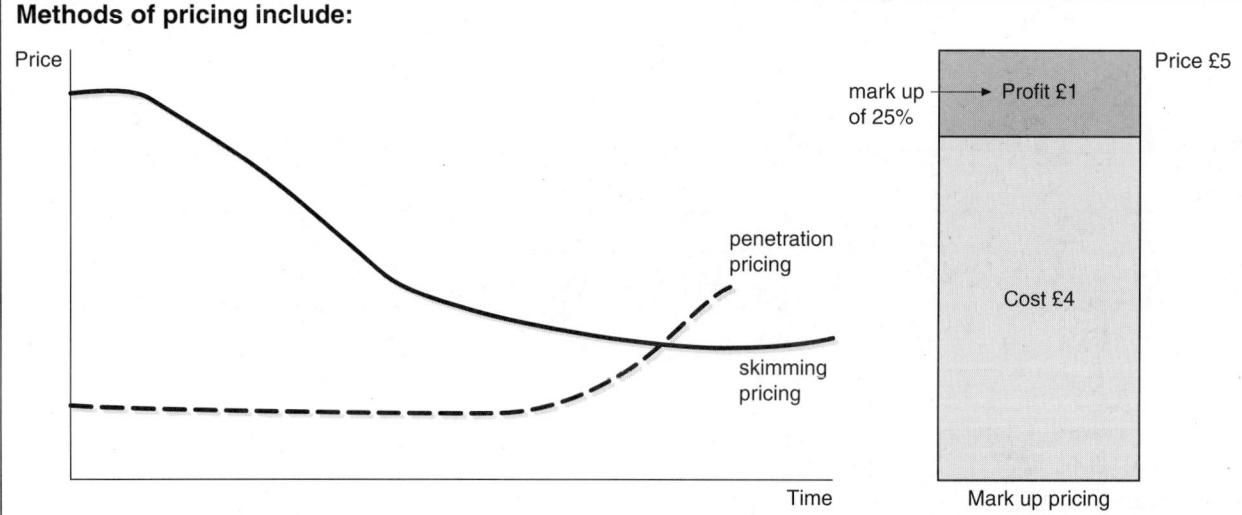

Skimming - high initial price to cover initial research and development costs quickly. Suitable for an innovative or protected product (e.g. a patent) and where demand is price inelastic

Penetration - low price to gain market share quickly. Suitable when there are substantial economies of scale or when demand is price sensitive

Competitor based - suitable when the market is competitive and price comparisons are easy, e.g. shopping goods

Demand based or perceived value - firm tries to estimate what people are willing to pay. This is the most market oriented approach, but it can be difficult to discover what people are willing to pay.

Cost based pricing - the firm adds an amount on to costs to decide on the price, i.e it adds a mark up on to the costs. This is a simple and, therefore, popular pricing method, but ignores demand conditions (see diagram).

Predatory pricing - a firm undercuts competitors to remove competition; once competitors leave, the price is increased again. This policy can lead to a price war in which all firms try to undercut each other.

Price discrimination - charging different prices for the same product/service, e.g. some taxis charge different prices late at night, rail fares are often higher at peak times; and some bars have 'happy hours' when drinks are cheaper. The firm will increase the price in segments where demand is price inelastic and decrease the price when demand is price elastic.

Loss leader - product sold below cost to generate orders for other product e.g. retailers put well known brand in shop windows and sell at a loss to attract people into the store.

Psychological pricing - focuses on consumer's perception of price, e.g. charging high prices to convey quality, charging £2.99 rather than £3.00 because people regard it as 'over £2' rather than in the £3 band, and stressing a reduction in price (e.g. was £20, now £12).

Product

Element of the marketing mix

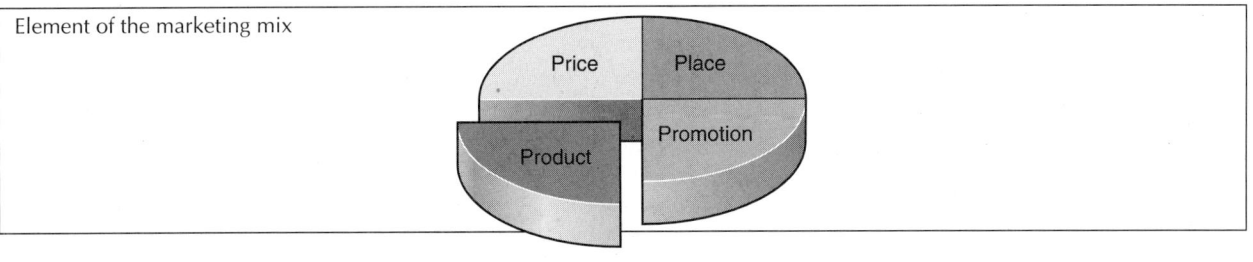

- performance - e.g the speed of a car, the power of a microwave
- features - the extras, e.g air conditioning or sunroof on a car
- aesthetics - What does it look like?
- brand name
- The quality of a product depends on its
- ease of manufacture
- durability - How long will it last?
- ease of servicing - How easy is it to fix?
- economics - What does it cost to produce? Can it be sold at a profit?
- reliability - How likely is it to go wrong in, say, the first year?

Product differentiation: anything which distinguishes the product from another in the eyes of the consumer

Product cannibalisation: when the sales of one product which a firm has launched reduce the sales of another of its existing products.

Packaging can

- protect the product from damage
- differentiate the product
- appeal to the consumer
- enhance the brand image.

Marketing 21

Product continued

Consumer goods: bought by the end user (i.e. the person who will consume them), e.g. carpets or washing machine.

Convenience items
Consumer searches for nearest shop and does not take long thinking about the purchase decision.
Extensive distribution.

Types include:

staple items - regularly bought, e.g. milk, newspaper

emergency items, e.g. plasters

impulse items: chewing gum - consumer did not go in to buy; afterthought

Shopping goods
Consumer shops around, e.g. for tv, washing machine
Often distributed in city centres

Consumers take time to buy; think about it; compare goods and prices; look for the best value

Speciality goods
unique/'special' goods; consumers willing to make special effort to buy, e.g. Porsche, Armani suits.

Exclusive distribution.

Durables: can be used several times, e.g. television

Non durables: can only be used once, e.g. food, matches

Producer goods: bought for use in the production process (i.e. to help make something else), e.g. raw materials or equipment.

Raw Materials - e.g. oranges, oil. Prices may fluctuate with supply and demand; often traded on world-wide markets. Little distinction between products; limited branding.

Manufactured parts - usually sold directly to manufacturer; price and service very important; branding and advertising less important.

Supplies - e.g light bulbs, soap. Little time spent in purchase; bought from intermediaries; price important; little brand preference.

Installations - capital goods, e.g. factories or new production equipment; long purchasing process; personal selling is important; often a long negotiation period; the technical aspects of the product are vital; price inelastic. Bought direct from manufacturer. Sellers have to be willing to design to order.

Accessory equipment - e.g desks. Often bought from wholesalers; competitive market; buyers likely to 'shop around'. many buyers; small orders.

	Producer goods	**Consumer goods**
Number of customers	Relatively few, professional buyers	Many
Relations with customers	Close	Often distant
Promotion	Often personal selling	Advertising more important
Distribution	Direct; few if any intermediaries	More intermediaries

---

Copyright: creator's or legal owner's rights in creative works such as paintings, writings, photographs or TV commercials. Copyright occurs automatically and does not need registering.

Trademark: a symbol used by a producer to identify a product which is legally protected under Trade Marks Act 1938. Trade Marks (amendment) Act 1984: trademarks registered with Patent Office.

Patent: a licence which prevents the copying of an idea; aims to protect inventors of a new product or process. New inventions protected for 15 years. Must be registered with Patent Office. This protection encourages research, allows inventors monopoly profits to reward their ideas, and encourages more products to be developed.

The American Can Co.'s patent for the ring pull has earned them over £50m.

Logo: visual symbol of a product or organisation e.g. Shell's 'shell'; Apple's 'apple', MGM's lion.

Distribution

The channel of distribution describes how the title of ownership passes from the manufacturer to the consumer.

Element of the marketing mix.

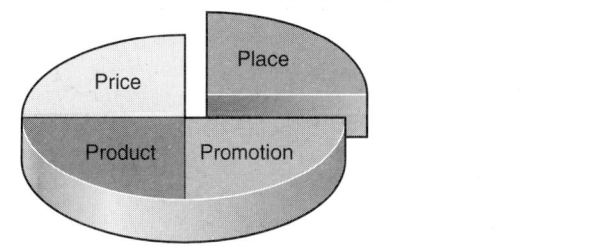

Levels of distribution

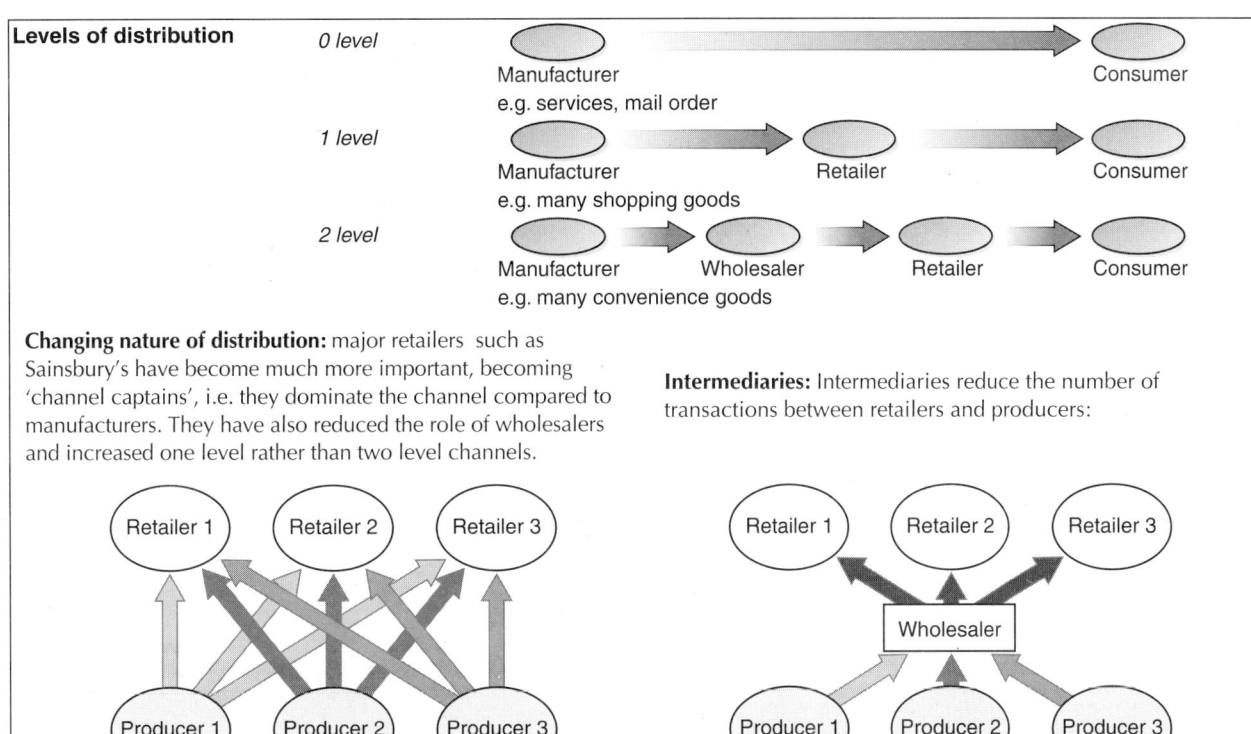

Changing nature of distribution: major retailers such as Sainsbury's have become much more important, becoming 'channel captains', i.e. they dominate the channel compared to manufacturers. They have also reduced the role of wholesalers and increased one level rather than two level channels.

Intermediaries: Intermediaries reduce the number of transactions between retailers and producers:

Choosing a distribution channel:

- Costs
- Alternatives - when Avon could not distribute cosmetics through department stores it sold door to door.
- Type of product - industrial products tend to have shorter channels as they have fewer customers and a more complex product which needs detailed explanation. Fragile products are also likely to have a direct channel. Basic low value items with many consumers widely spread geographically are likely to have long channels with many intermediaries.

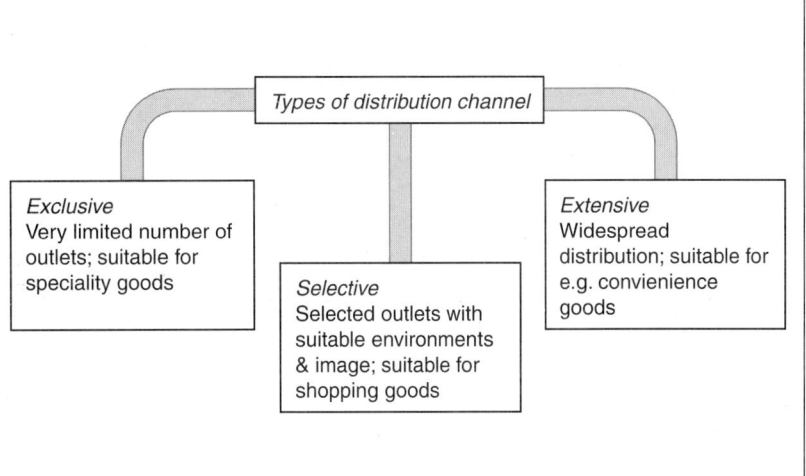

Intermediaries

Wholesalers: 'break bulk' i.e. buy in large quantities from manufacturers and break into smaller quantities for retailers.

Agents: do not take ownership of the goods. They represent a firm and try to gain sales for it. Receive a commission. Often used to enter overseas markets.

Marketing 23

Distribution continued

Wholesalers and manufacturers
Wholesalers buy in bulk from the manufacturer. This means the manufacturer does not keep as many stocks. The wholesaler will also promote the manufacturer's products to try to sell them to the retailers.

By selling to wholesalers, the manufacturer receives cash more quickly and no longer has the risk of the goods not being sold.

Wholesalers and retailers
The wholesaler buys in large quantities from manufacturers and then sells in smaller quantities to the retailers. The retailer can select goods from a range of manufacturers from the wholesaler. The wholesaler can also keep the retailer informed of the latest developments by the manufacturer.

Recent developments
Increasingly retailers are buying direct from the manufacturer. This is because the retailers have grown in size and taken on many of the roles of wholesalers.

Transport
This is a key element of distribution. The choice of transport depends on:
- how important it is to get the goods to their destinations quickly
- how much each option costs
- the nature of the product e.g. is it fragile? expensive? heavy?

Options:

- road - most frequent form of transport within the UK; fairly cheap and fast; can deliver door to door; can send at any time (no set timetables). Firms may deliver themselves or hire a road haulage company.

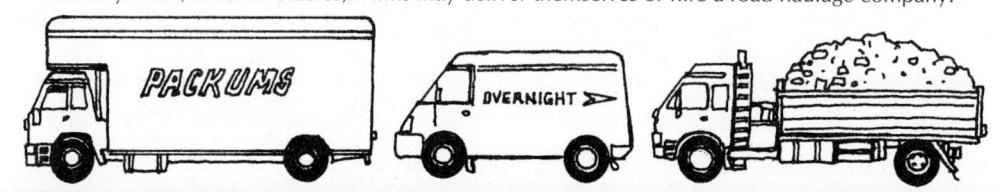

- railways - used for moving bulky goods long distances.

- air and sea - used mainly for international transport. Air transport is expensive but fast over long distances. Sea transport (such as cargo ships and oil tankers) is used for bulky items.

24 Marketing

Promotion

Promotion involves communication about the product or service.

Element of the marketing mix.

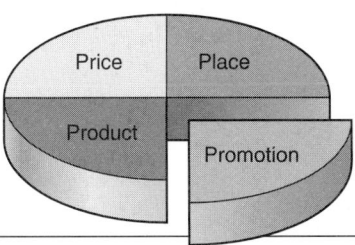

Objectives may be:
- to make consumers aware of, e.g. new product launch
- to remind consumers
- to persuade consumers

Methods of promoting

- **Sale promotion:** short term incentives to increase sales, e.g. free samples, coupons, competitions. Effect is often to destroy loyalty to other brands and encourage brand switching; when promotion ends consumers often switch to another brand's offer. Sales promotion is called below the line promotional activity.

- **Advertising:** paid for communication. It is called an 'above the line' promotional activity.

- **Public relations:** involves managing relations with different publics, e.g. the media, consumers, pressure groups, investors. May involve getting media coverage of event or product launch or generally creating a favourable impression and generating word of mouth interest. The difficulty is that it is not easy to control what others write or say.

- **Personal selling:** use of sales representatives.

- **Direct mailing:** information is sent through the post

- **Exhibitions and trade fairs**

- **Merchandising:** an attempt to influence consumers at point of sale, e.g. display material

- **Packaging:** e.g. design, shape, information displayed on it

- **Branding:** name or design which identifies the products or services of a manufacturer and distinguishes them from competitors.

- **Sponsorship:** firms finance events, e.g. firms sponsor sports events to attract publicity.

Brands

Own label (own brand) - retailers use own name (e.g. Sainsbury's), rather than a manufacturer's.

Family brand - business name on a number of products, e.g. Heinz beans, soup, spaghetti

Individual product branding, i.e. each product has a different brand name, e.g. Van den Bergh produces Flora, Delight, Krona, Stork, Blue Brand and Echo margarines.

Brand leader - brand with the highest market share

Using the promotional mix

Industrial goods are generally sold to a few professional buyers. Advertising is less important apart from, e.g. the trade press, whereas personal selling is vital.

With consumer goods, such as jeans, advertising to the final consumer is more common. Personal selling is important to get the items distributed but advertising pulls the consumers into the shops.

Marketing 25

Advertising

Advertising agency: designs and produces adverts for a firm.

They usually employ copywriters to write the text, artists to draw illustrations and designers.

The agency will develop the message of the advert and advertise on the most appropriate medium e.g. TV, radio, newspapers. They will also help to plan the campaign e.g. plan the timing and frequency of adverts.

When constructing an advertising campaign consider:

- the advertising budget
- the target audience
- the most appropriate medium

Advertising should seek to :

A *attract attention*   I *create interest*
D *develop a desire*   A *lead to action (purchase)*

(the **AIDA** model)

Advertising occurs on posters, in newspapers, in magazines, on television, and on the radio.

When deciding on the appropriate medium, advertisers should consider: the cost, the target audience, and the appropriateness of the chosen medium.

Controls on advertising:

1. Advertising Standards Authority is a voluntary body which seeks to ensure adverts are 'legal decent honest, truthful and do not cause widespread offence'.

2. Independent Television Commission - controls advertising on tv and radio.

Corporate advertising: promoting the company as a whole rather than a particular product

Arguments for advertising
- informs
- increases sales
- creates jobs
- creative/art form

Arguments against
- adds 'unnecessary' costs
- persuades people to buy goods /services they do not really want
- encourages the 'wrong' kind of values and behaviour, e.g. greed

Types of advertising

Informative advertising - this lets people know what the company is offering

Persuasive advertising - this tries to persuade the customer to switch from another product or to buy more

Advertising media

- television: expensive but adverts can have colour, movement and sound; adverts usually quite brief and difficult to reach a particular target group

- radio: relatively cheap

- printed adverts: generally more long term than the TV or the radio, e.g. newspaper adverts can be cut out and kept for reference. BUT printed adverts generally have less impact than TV advertising.

Printed adverts include:

- national press: fairly expensive (but cheaper than TV); good means of providing information; can target particular age and income groups. National newspapers are divided into quality papers (e.g. *The Times, The Daily Telegraph* and *The Independent*) and the tabloids (e.g. *The Sun, The Star*). There are also regional and local newspapers.

- magazines: cheap and effective means of reaching a particular target group

- local press: relatively cheap

- posters: effective if a good location can be found; usually looked at very quickly

- leaflets: firms can have leaflets delivered to people's houses in a particular area.

Sources of Finance

Short term finance: for day to day requirements: Overdraft- very flexible; interest paid when the account is overdrawn and usually lower than a bank loan. However, amount owed can be demanded back at any moment.

Medium term finance:
- Bank loan - borrowed over a fixed period of time. Loan is repaid in regular installments.
- Hire purchase - often used to buy equipment. Usually involves a down payment and then regular installments. This is a way of spreading the payments for an item although it is more expensive overall because of interest payments.
- Trade credit - buying items from suppliers and paying later, e.g. 30 days.
- Leasing - equipment is rented. This avoids a large initial outflow and equipment may be repaired and updated easily.
- Debt factoring - firms borrow money using their debtors (i.e. the amount owed) as security. Debt factor lends to firm and takes over responsibility for debtors.

Long term finance:
- Issue share capital - may involve more owners and loss of control; shares may be sold to existing shareholders (rights issue), to general public (public or direct issue), to merchant bank which then sells them to general public (offer for sale) or to private clients (placing).
- Debentures - IOU certificates; the buyer is paid interest each year and receives the amount they lent back after a fixed period of time; the buyer is not an owner of the company.
- Mortgage - borrowings using property as collateral (security) to guarantee the loan.
- Government assistance - e.g. grants.
- Venture capital - money lent to small firms (usually combination of loans and share capital) to finance new firms which are risky and may have difficulty getting finance from elsewhere.

Sources of internal finance
- Retained profit
- Sale of assets
- Working capital (e.g. reduce stocks, limit credit to customers)

Sources of external finance
- Sale of shares
- Loans
- Debt factoring
- Credit from suppliers

Loans v shares

Problems of loans
- Interest must be paid before owners receive dividends
- Lenders can force liquidation
- Higher risk - interest must be paid, even if profits are low

Problems of selling shares
- Lose ownership and control with new investors
- Owners expect dividends although may be possible to delay

Accounts

Accounts: numerate information to help decision making. Accounting collects data on a firm's activities, turns this into monetary values; and presents findings in a suitable form for the decision maker.

Accounting information is used by
- outsiders e.g. potential investors, lenders, government, suppliers
- insiders e.g. managers, employees

Types of accounting

Financial accounting: essentially backward looking; mainly concerned with record keeping

Management accounting: to aid management's decisions and planning; concerned with the future, e.g. what price to set?

Accountants
- keep a record of the firm's transactions
- help to keep control over the firm's finances
- analyse the financial implications of any decision
- present financial information e.g. to other managers

Accounting principles

Realisation: a sale is realised when a good is delivered; i.e. when goods are delivered they can be recorded as revenue even if cash has not been received.

Accruals: costs must be matched to the period when they are incurred, e.g. if a firm buys £300 of materials and only uses up a third in this period, the costs are £100; £200 is left in stock.

Materiality: deciding whether an item is worth treating as an asset and depreciating, e.g. if only a third of a £1.50 jar of coffee has been used by the end of the period, the cost should be entered as 50p and the remaining value of the asset recorded as £1. However, items as small are this are often 'written off', i.e. all of the £1.50 would be put as a cost in one go. This is because they are not material enough for a firm to bother measuring exactly how much has been used up.

Conservatism or Prudence: accountants should be conservative when producing accounts; if in doubt they should underestimate revenue and overestimate costs.

Consistency: accounting information should be consistently gathered and presented from one year to the next, e.g. a firm should not simply change its depreciation policies from one year to another just to make its results look better.

The accounting profession and the interpretation and development of accounting principles is regulated in the UK by the Accounting Standards Board (ASB).

The ASB is responsible for producing:

FRED Financial Reporting Exposure Drafts - draft versions of proposed new accounting standards

FRS Financial Reporting Standards - agreed accounting standards.

Balance sheet

> **Balance sheet:** shows the financial position of an organisation at a particular moment in time. It shows what the business owns and how this has been financed.

Balance sheet for a company as at (a certain date)

This is what the company owns

- **Fixed Assets:** *provide a benefit for more than 12 months*
  - Tangible - e.g. buildings, factories
  - Intangible - e.g. brand name, goodwill, patents
  - Financial - e.g. investments in other firms

- **Current Assets:** *provide a benefit for less than 12 months*
  - Stock - e.g. raw materials, works in progress, finished goods
  - Debtors - the amount owed to the firm; also prepayments (advance payments)
  - Cash - (or money in the bank)

TOTAL ASSETS

These are the sources of finance

- **Current Liabilities** — e.g. creditors of less than one year, overdraft, tax and dividends due
- **Long Term Liabilities** (creditors of more than a year) — e.g. loans
- **Reserves** — e.g. retained profit
- **Issued shares**

TOTAL LIABILITIES AND SHAREHOLDER FUNDS

These items can be rearranged to give:

Balance Sheet as at (a certain date)

Fixed Assets

plus Current Assets
less Current Liabilities } *Called* **'Working capital'** *or* **'Net current assets'**

= **ASSETS EMPLOYED or NET ASSETS**

Long term Liabilities
plus Reserves
plus Issued Share Capital

= **CAPITAL EMPLOYED**

CAPITAL EMPLOYED	→	ASSETS EMPLOYED
Long term sources of finance	Used to acquire	e.g. buildings, factories, stocks, cash

Finance 29

Balance sheet continued

If the business is not a company, the balance sheet will be slightly different e.g:

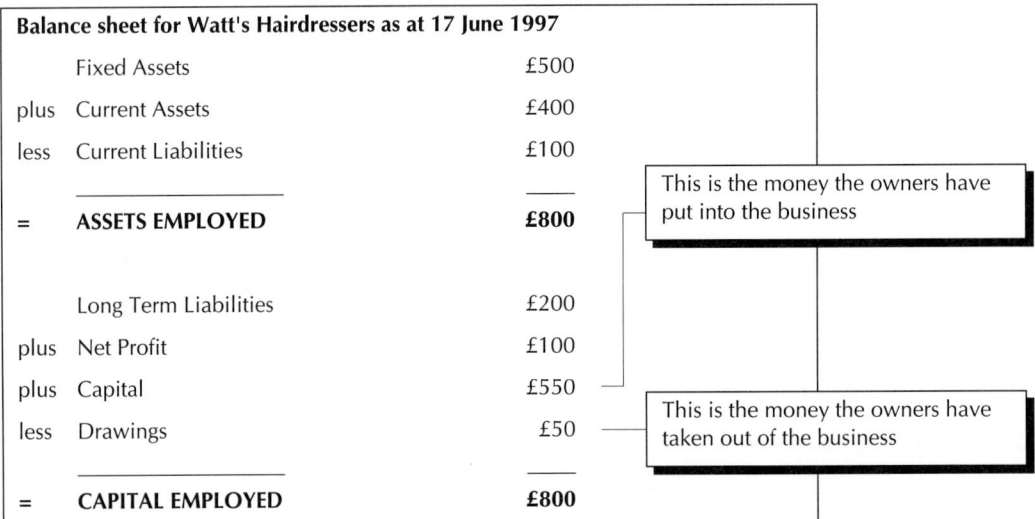

Examples of Assets and Liabilities

Items of interest on the balance sheet include

Debtors:
These appear as current assets in balance sheet. An analyst should try to find out more about who owes the firm money, e.g. if the money is all owed by one firm it may be riskier than if it is owed by several firms. It would also be useful to have details of the track record of the debtors, and information about how long they have owed the company money, e.g 2 days? or 11 months?

Reserves:
These include retained profits. The reserves figure records the total profit the firm has made up until now. Remember that reserves are not all sitting in cash; they will also be held in other forms of assets such as stock and buildings.

Working capital; also called 'Net current assets':
This involves the day to day finance of the organisation. It is measured by current assets minus current liabilities

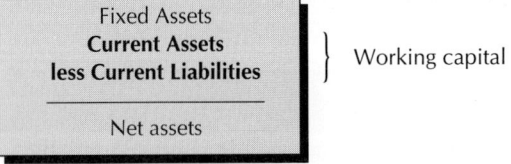

The management of working capital includes:
- minimising time lags between input of resources and payments for sold goods and services.
- minimising stock levels whilst still holding enough to continue production and sales.

30 Finance

Depreciation

Fixed assets

FIXED ASSETS + CURRENT ASSETS = TOTAL ASSETS

A fixed asset will depreciate over time. Depreciation is the cost of a fixed asset. It is entered each year in the profit and loss account and reduces the value of the asset on the balance sheet.

If an asset is bought for £500 and it is estimated it will be sold for £100 after 4 years it will cost the firm £400. A decision must be made about how to allocate this cost. The simplest method is to allocate it in equal amounts i.e. £100 each year. This is the STRAIGHT LINE METHOD of depreciation.

Year	Value of asset on balance sheet (called net book value) £	Annual cost of asset (depreciation) (appears on profit and loss) £	Accumulated depreciation £
0	500	0	0
1	400	100	100
2	300	100	200
3	200	100	300
4	100	100	400

Historic cost = original cost of the asset

Accumulated depreciation = total depreciation to date.

Net book value = historic cost minus accumulated depreciation, i.e. value of asset left on balance sheet.

Residual value = value of asset at the end of its life, i.e on disposal

Another method of depreciation is called the REDUCING BALANCE METHOD. Using this method the asset loses value more rapidly in the early years compared to the later years.

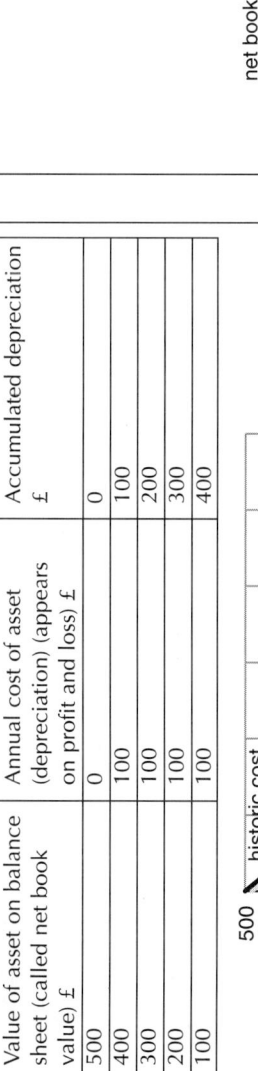

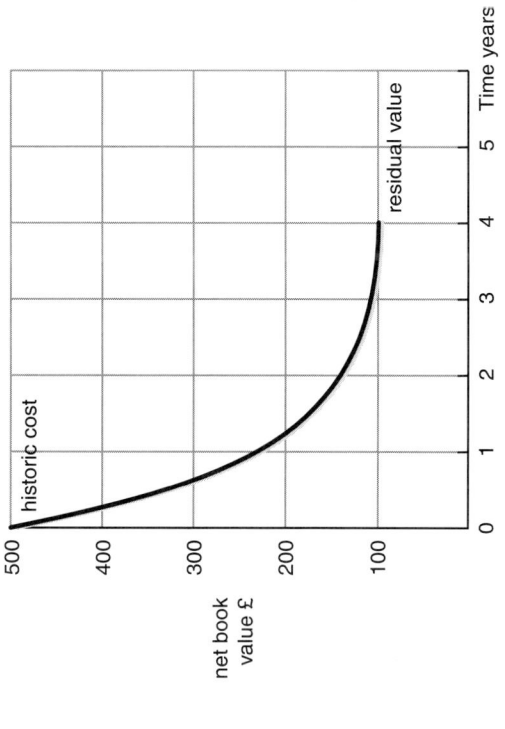

The reducing balance method depreciates the assets by a constant percentage (not a constant amount) each year. This means that the cost entered on the profit and loss is higher in the earlier years and lower in the later years than using the straight line method. The reducing balance method is harder to calculate than the straight line method but is more appropriate if assets lose value quickly in their early years.

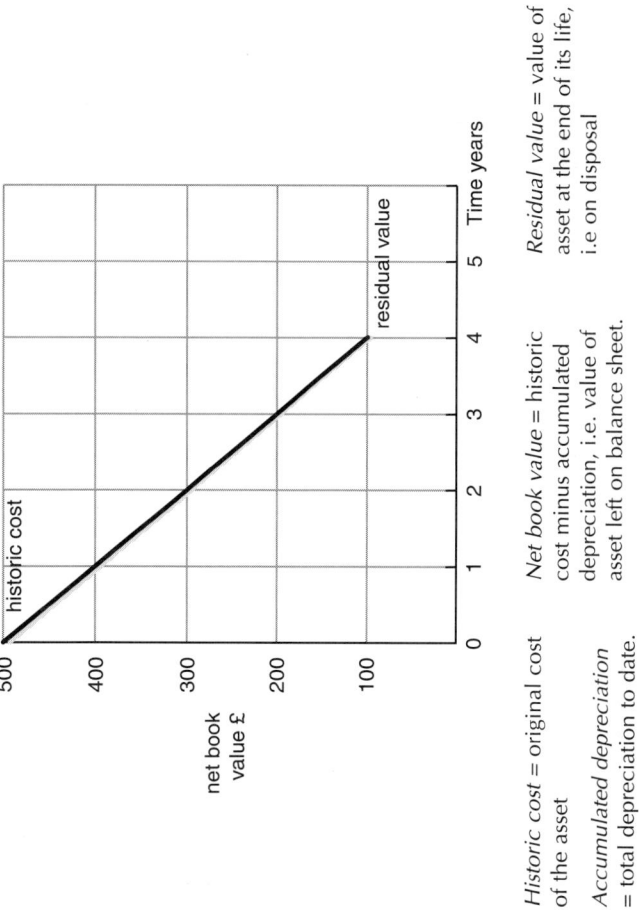

Finance 31

Profit and loss statement

Profit and loss statement: shows the profit or loss generated over a given period.

It involves: **Revenue or Turnover** - this measures the value of the sales; it may not be in cash since the firm is often owed money (debtors).

Costs - this is the value of items used up in the process; this is not necessarily the same as the cash paid out; e.g. if firm pays for £300 of materials in cash but only uses up one third, the costs are £100 since the other £200 of materials remain as assets of the firm.

Profit and loss

Gross profit is the difference between sales and the costs of the products sold ('cost of sales').

Cost of sales

The cost of sales is the cost of producing the items which have been sold (in manufacturing) or the cost of the goods bought to be sold in the shop (in retailing). It also includes an adjustment for the number of stocks used up. e.g. if the firm made 10 units for £200 but also sold another 5 units which were in stock and had cost £100 to make, the cost of sales is for all 15 units (i.e. £200 + £100 = £300).

Expenses

These are costs of running the firm such as wages, rent, electricity and selling costs. They also include:

- depreciation - this is the cost of the wear and tear of fixed assets such as machinery. As the firm produces, the equipment is used up and the firm calculates this as a cost.
- bad debts - if customers do not pay up, the firm has a bad debt. This will be written off, i.e. put as a cost in the profit and loss.

Net profit is gross profit less overheads.

Profit and Loss Statement for the year ending 1997

	Sales	£200
less	Cost of sales	£140
=	**GROSS PROFIT**	**£60**
less	Expenses	
	Wages	£10
	Rent and electricity	£10
	Depreciation of equipment	£15
		£5
=	**NET PROFIT**	**£20**

Profit & cash

Profit is not the same as cash: e.g. If goods are sold on credit this creates revenue but no cash. If materials or equipment are bought in cash, this leads to a cash outflow, but no cost is involved until they are used up. Imagine a £450 asset is purchased for cash, is used for four years, and is then sold for £50. The overall cost is £400 (£450 - £50). Using the straight line method of depreciation, the cost is £100 p.a.

Year	0	1	2	3	4
Cash flows £	(450)	0	0	0	50
Costs £ annual depreciation	0	100	100	100	100

Profit v. cash example:

A firm buys £300 of materials in cash and uses up £200 of them to produce goods which are sold on credit for £1000. Labour is paid £50 in cash. No other costs are involved.

	£			£
Turnover	1000	Cash in		0
Costs (labour)	50	cash out (labour)		50
(materials)	200	250	(materials)	300
Profit		750	Cash		(350)

Revenue v. Capital items

Revenue items appear on the profit and loss. Capital items appear on the balance sheet. If, for example, a firm purchases equipment, this is an asset and appears on the balance sheet (capital item). If a firm uses up materials this is a cost and appears on the profit and loss (revenue item). Sometimes there is debate about an item, e.g. research and development. Some firms treat this as an investment, list on the balance sheet and depreciate it over a number of years. Others 'write it off' in one year, i.e treat it as something which has been used up and so put it all as a cost in one go (revenue item).

Examples

Revenue items	Capital items
Wages	Equipment
Materials	Property
	Transport e.g. vehicles

Gross profit margin: (gross profit/sales) × 100

e.g. $(\frac{60}{200}) \times 100 = 30\%$

Net profit margin: (net profit/sales) × 100

e.g. $(\frac{20}{200}) \times 100 = 10\%$

32 Finance

Ratios

Ratio analysis compares one figure with another to place it in context and assess its relative importance. It helps analyse data and aids decision making.

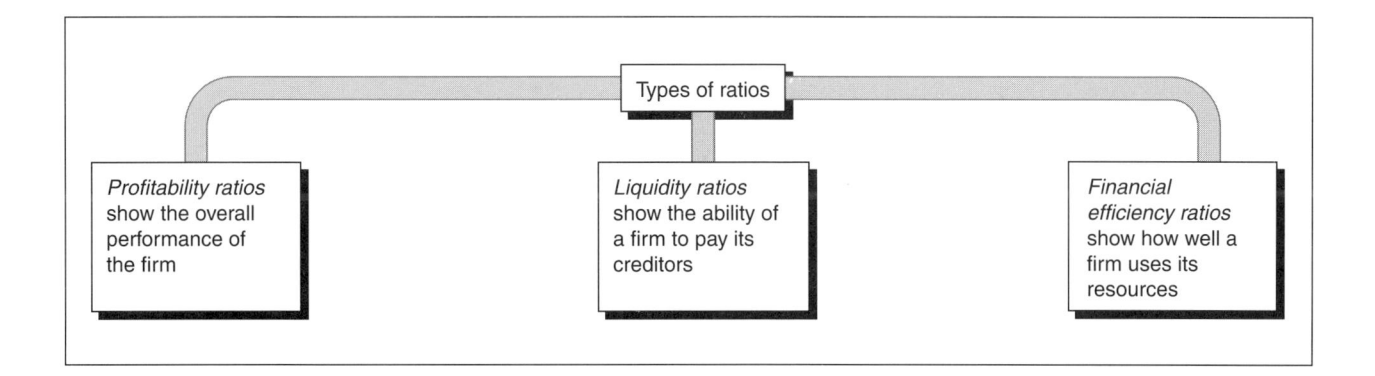

```
                        Types of ratios
           ┌───────────────────┼───────────────────┐
  Profitability ratios   Liquidity ratios    Financial
  show the overall       show the ability of  efficiency ratios
  performance of         a firm to pay its    show how well a
  the firm               creditors            firm uses its
                                              resources
```

Profitability ratios: measure how well the firm is doing. One of the most common is

return on capital employed (%) = $\dfrac{\text{net profit}}{\text{capital employment}} \times 100$

Assuming firms are aiming for profit, the higher the ratio the better. It measures the rate of return being generated by managers and can be compared to other rates of return, e.g. interest rates in banks.

The overall return depends on the value of the sales and how much profit is made per sale

- The gross profit per sale is measured by the

  gross profit margin (%) = $\dfrac{\text{gross profit}}{\text{sales}} \times 100$

- The net profit per sales is measured by the

  net profit margin (%) = $\dfrac{\text{net profit}}{\text{sales}} \times 100$

Assessing profitability

To assess its profitability the firm must consider:

- is it better than in the past?
- is it more than competitors are earning?
- does it provide enough funds for investment?
- does it provide enough rewards for the owners?

Increasing profitability

To increase its profitability the firm could:

- cut the price and hope the increase in sales compensates for the lower profit per unit
- increase the price and hope the fall in sales does not outweigh the gains from a higher profit per sale
- cut costs, but quality (and so sales) may suffer
- focus on the more profitable products; drop the unprofitable or less profitable ones.

Liquidity ratios: measure the ability of an organisation to meet its short term liabilities.

Working Capital Ratio *(also called Current Ratio)* $\dfrac{\text{Current Asset}}{\text{Current Liabilities}}$ (Typically 1.5 or 2)

Liquidity Ratio *(also called Acid Test Ratio)* $\dfrac{\text{Current Assets without stocks}}{\text{Current Liabilities}}$

The Acid Test is a tighter test of liquidity than the Current Ratio. It measures the ability of the firm to meet its Current Liabilities if it could not sell its stock. Usually between 0.8 and 1.

Finance 33

Ratios continued

Financial efficiency ratios: show how well the firm is using its resources

Stock turnover measures the value of the firm's stock compared to its sales. Stock turnover = $\dfrac{\text{Cost of sales}}{\text{Average stock}}$

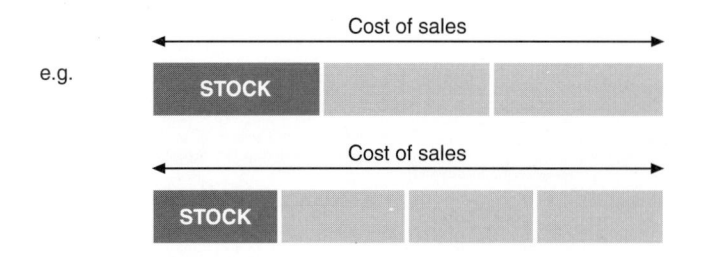

e.g.

Stock will be used up 3 times. Stock turnover is 3.

Stock turnover = 4.

To calculate average stock use:

$$\dfrac{\text{Stock at start of the period + Stock at end of the period}}{2}$$

Example
If stock at the beginning of the year was worth £100 and stock at the end of the year was worth £300 then,

average stock = $\dfrac{£100 + £300}{2}$ = £200

If cost of sales is £800 then stock turnover = $\dfrac{800}{200}$ = 4

> Stock turnover shows how many times stock is used up during the year. The higher the figure the more times it is used up. In recent years many firms have tried to reduce the amount of stock they hold to cut stockholding costs. This increases the stock turnover ratio.

Debtor collection period (Debtor days)

This measures the amount of debtors in relation to the turnover.

Debtor days = $\dfrac{\text{Debtors}}{\text{Turnover}} \times 365$

For example, if debtors are £100 and turnover is £400

Debtor days = $\dfrac{100}{400} \times 365$ = 91.25 days

The firm is owed the equivalent of 91.25 days worth of sales. The larger this number the more the firm is owed.

Creditor period

This measures the firm's creditors compared to its cost of sales.

Creditor days = $\dfrac{\text{Creditors}}{\text{Cost of sales}} \times 365$

For example, if creditors are £50 and cost of sales are £300

Creditor days = $\dfrac{50}{300} \times 365$ = 60.83 days

The firm owes the equivalent of 60.83 days of its cost of sales. The larger this number is the more the firm owes.

Limitations to ratio analysis

- Ratios are only as reliable as the underlying data, i.e. if the accounts have been 'massaged' to create a favourable impression, then the ratios may also flatter. In addition, ratios are often calculated using out of date information, e.g. data from last year's accounts. Ratio analysis based on past data will not necessarily help predict the future.
- They only use quantitative data. Also need to consider qualitative factors, such as the skill of management, the rate of change in the market, and the industrial relations record.
- Need to consider the type of firm, stage in its development, and the objectives of the owners, e.g a low profitability ratio may be acceptable in the early stages of growth when the owners are investing heavily in equipment and training.
- Typicality - the figures in the balance sheet show a particular day; this may not be typical and consequently any ratios calculated using these figures are not necessarily representative.
- Need to consider what the ratios are for other firms (inter firm comparison) and what ratios have been in the past (intra firm comparison), e.g. a 12% ROCE may seem high but it is not as impressive if others are earning 14% and last year the firm earned 16%.
- Need to consider the context, e.g. Is the market growing or declining? Is the economy booming or not? For example we expect profitability to be higher in a growing market.

Auditors report: companies must get independent accountants to check their accounts; they produce an auditors' report. This usually states that in their opinion the annual accounts represent a 'true and fair view'.

Ratios example

Balance Sheet
as at 17th June 1997   £
Fixed Assets   **190**
Current Assets
stocks   10
debtors   6
cash   4   20
less
Current Liabilities
Creditors   10   **10**

Assets Employed (or Net Assets)   **200**

Issued share capital of £1 shares   100
Reserves   50
Long Term Liabilities   50

Capital Employed   **200**

Profit and loss for the year ending 17th June 1997
                                                  £
turnover (or sales)   400
cost of sales   300
gross profit   **100**
expenses   80
net profit   **20**

---

ratio	equation	measurement	workings	answer
return on capital employed	$\left(\dfrac{\text{net profit}}{\text{capital employed}}\right) \times 100$	%	$\left(\dfrac{20}{200}\right) \times 100$	10%
gross profit margin	$\left(\dfrac{\text{gross profit}}{\text{turnover}}\right) \times 100$	%	$\left(\dfrac{100}{400}\right) \times 100$	25%
net profit margin	$\left(\dfrac{\text{net profit}}{\text{turnover}}\right) \times 100$	%	$\left(\dfrac{20}{400}\right) \times 100$	5%
working capital ratio (current ratio)	$\dfrac{\text{current assets}}{\text{current liabilities}}$	number of times	$\dfrac{20}{10}$	2
acid test ratio	$\dfrac{\text{current assets without stocks}}{\text{current liabilities}}$	number of times	$\dfrac{10}{10}$	1
stock turnover (stock turn)	$\dfrac{\text{cost of sales}}{\text{average stock}}$	number of times	$\dfrac{300}{10}$	30
debtor days (debtor collection period)	$\left(\dfrac{\text{debtors}}{\text{turnover}}\right) \times 365$	number of days	$\left(\dfrac{6}{400}\right) \times 365$	5.5 days
creditor days (creditor payment period)	$\left(\dfrac{\text{creditors}}{\text{cost of sales}}\right) \times 365$	number of days	$\left(\dfrac{10}{300}\right) \times 365$	12.2 days

Break-even

Break even is the output at which revenue equals costs, i.e. no profit or loss is made

- Total costs = fixed costs + variable costs
- Fixed costs do not change with output, e.g. rent
- Variable costs vary directly with output, e.g. materials
- Total revenue = price x quantity
- Profit = total revenue - total costs

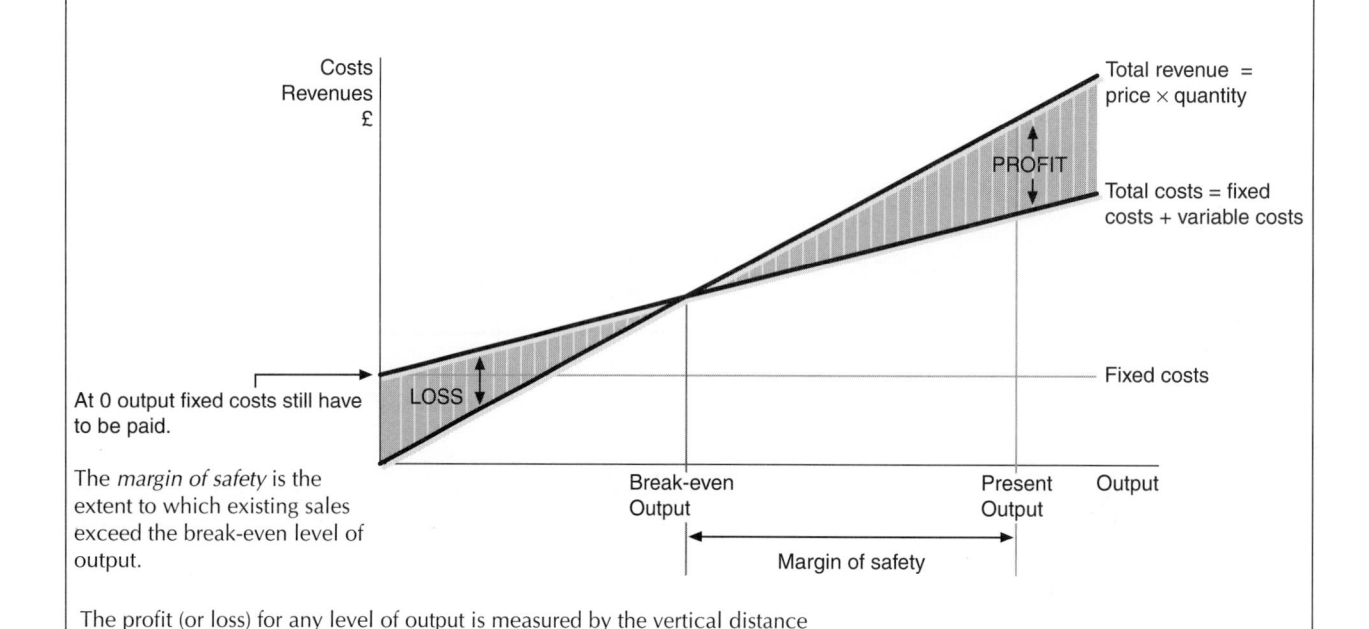

At 0 output fixed costs still have to be paid.

The *margin of safety* is the extent to which existing sales exceed the break-even level of output.

The profit (or loss) for any level of output is measured by the vertical distance between the total revenue and the total cost line

Types of costs

Variable costs: change directly with output, e.g. raw materials

Fixed costs: do not change with output, e.g. rent

Semi variable costs: vary with output but not directly, e.g. supervision costs, maintenance costs

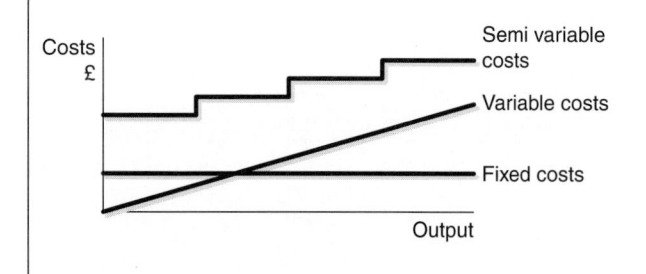

Fixed costs	Variable costs
Rent	Materials
Interest payments	Wages
Depreciation	

Direct costs: costs which can be identified with a particular cost centre (e.g a product or process) and which vary directly with activity or output, e.g. the materials used in one process or labour directly involved in one product

Indirect costs: costs which cannot be directly identified with a particular cost centre, e.g. general marketing costs or administration. Also called **overheads**.

Indirect costs may be fixed (e.g rent) or variable (e.g variable overheads such as maintenance costs; these are not directly associated with a cost centre, and, although more maintenance is likely to be needed with expansion, these costs will not change directly with output).

Plotting the break even graph: produce a table which calculates total costs and total revenue.

Example: Price per unit £10; Variable cost per unit £4; Fixed costs £12000; Maximum output 5000 units.

Quantity	Revenue (price × quantity) £	Fixed costs £	Variable costs (variable cost per unit × quantity) £	Total costs = fixed costs + variable costs £	Profit/loss £
0	0	12000	0	12000	(12000)
1000	10000	12000	4000	16000	(6000)
2000	20000	12000	8000	20000	0 = break-even
5000	50000	12000	20000	32000	18000

36 Finance

Plotted from previous table:

A break-even chart showing Revenue/Costs £ (0 to 50000) on the y-axis and Output (0 to 5000) on the x-axis. Total revenue line rises from origin to 50000 at output 5000. Total costs line (dashed) rises from about 12000 to about 32000. The two lines intersect at output 2000. The area to the left of intersection is labelled LOSS; the area to the right is labelled PROFIT.

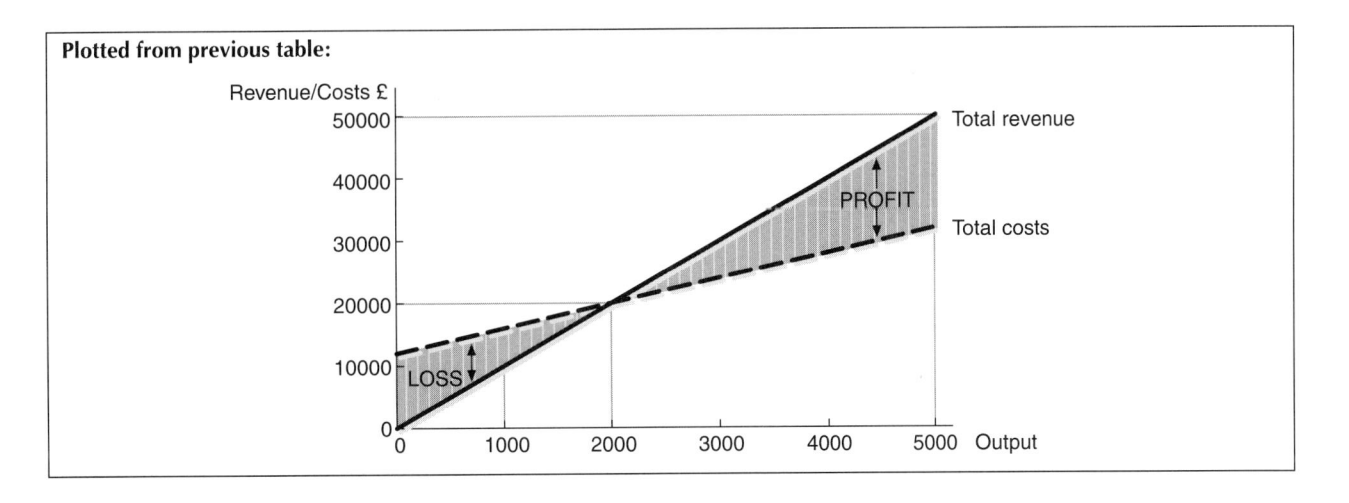

Break-even helps the firm to analyse what happens if:
- output is changed
- price is changed
- variable costs are changed
- fixed costs are changed

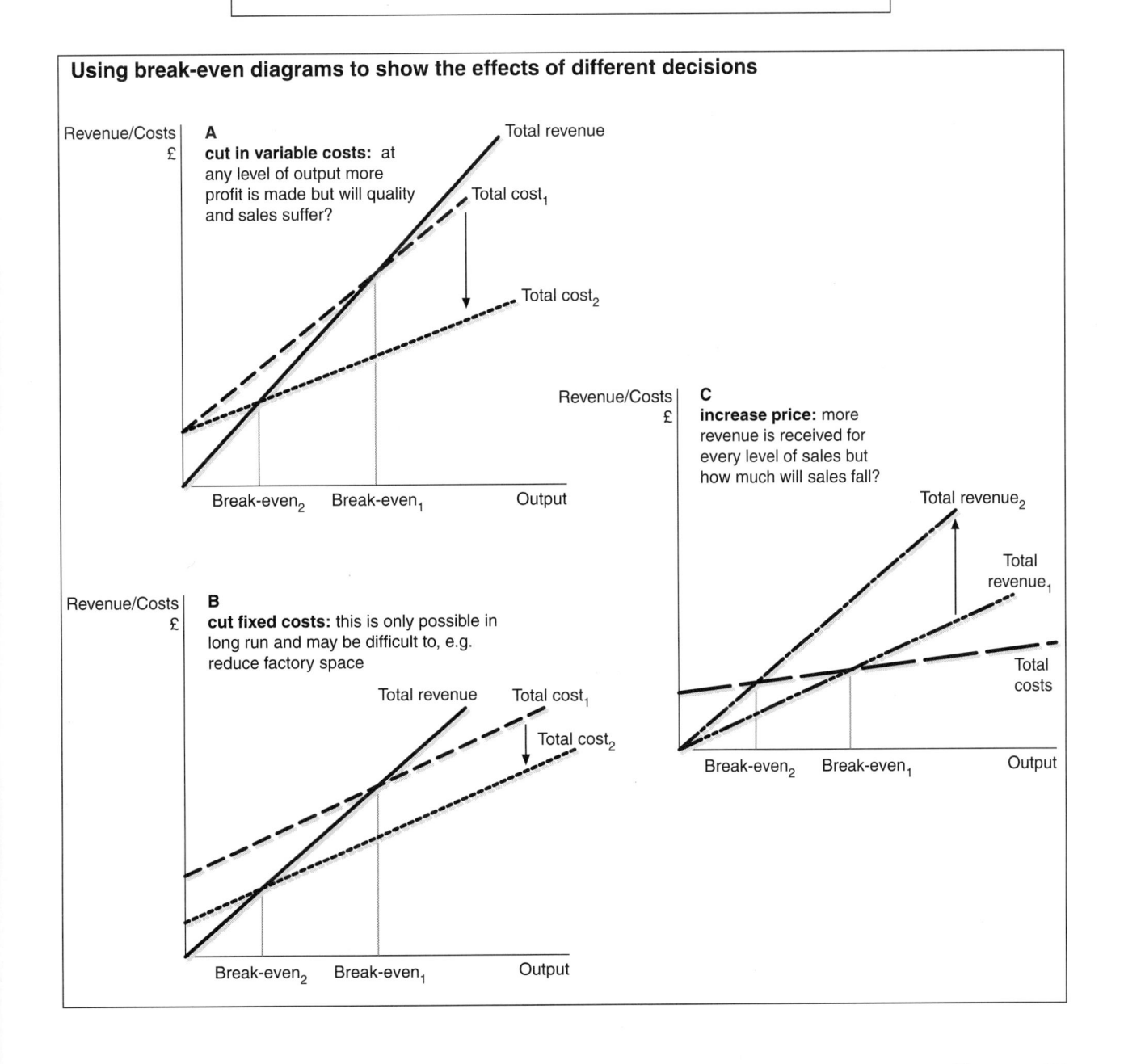

Using break-even diagrams to show the effects of different decisions

A cut in variable costs: at any level of output more profit is made but will quality and sales suffer?

Diagram shows Total revenue, Total cost₁, and Total cost₂ (lower slope). Break-even₂ is to the left of Break-even₁.

B cut fixed costs: this is only possible in long run and may be difficult to, e.g. reduce factory space

Diagram shows Total revenue, Total cost₁, and Total cost₂ (lower intercept). Break-even₂ is to the left of Break-even₁.

C increase price: more revenue is received for every level of sales but how much will sales fall?

Diagram shows Total revenue₂ (steeper), Total revenue₁, and Total costs. Break-even₂ is to the left of Break-even₁.

Budgets, forecasts and cash flow

A budget is a quantitative statement which covers a specific period and is usually expressed in financial terms.

Budgets:
- help planning
- help coordinate different activities so that, e.g. overall costs are not too high
- allocate responsibilities and communicate to subordinates what they have to achieve
- motivate employees by setting targets
- enable superiors to review performance by referring back to the set budget at the end of the period.

Types of budget:

Sales budget: sets sales estimates for each product in terms of number of units

Production budget: sets output targets

Cash budget: cash flow forecast

Master budget: summarises estimated income, expenditure, and profit.

Forecasts

A forecast is an estimate of a future situation. For example, a firm is likely to estimate

- **sales:** so that it can plan production and people requirements. If sales are expected to increase, the firm might need to expand its output and recruit more staff.
- **cashflow:** so that it can identify if it is likely to have cashflow problems. If a firm forecasts it will be short of cash it can try and make suitable plans. For example, it might try and arrange a loan.
- **profits:** by forecasting sales and costs the firm can estimate its future profits. If this level of profits is not high enough the firm can develop different plans. For example, it might try to increase its sales or cut costs.

A firm will regularly compare its forecasted figures with the actual results. For example, it will compare its actual sales with the level of sales it predicted. If the actual figures are different from the forecast the firm will investigate why. This should improve its future forecasting and helps to identify any unexpected changes in its markets or activities.

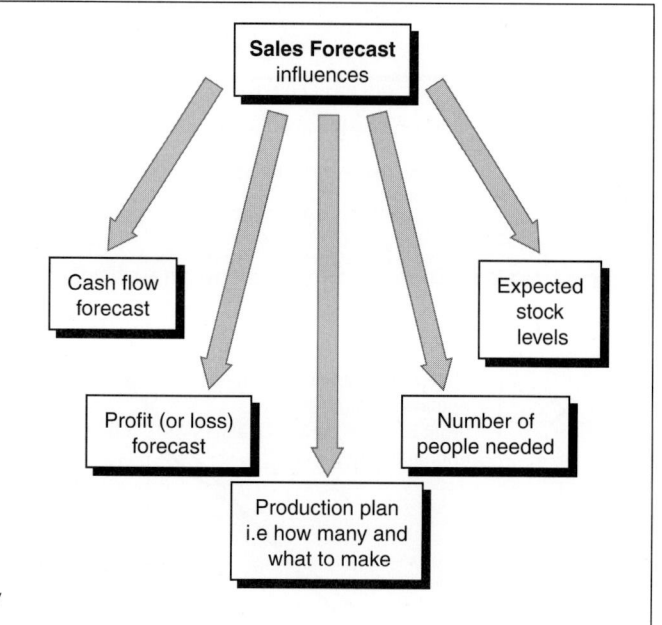

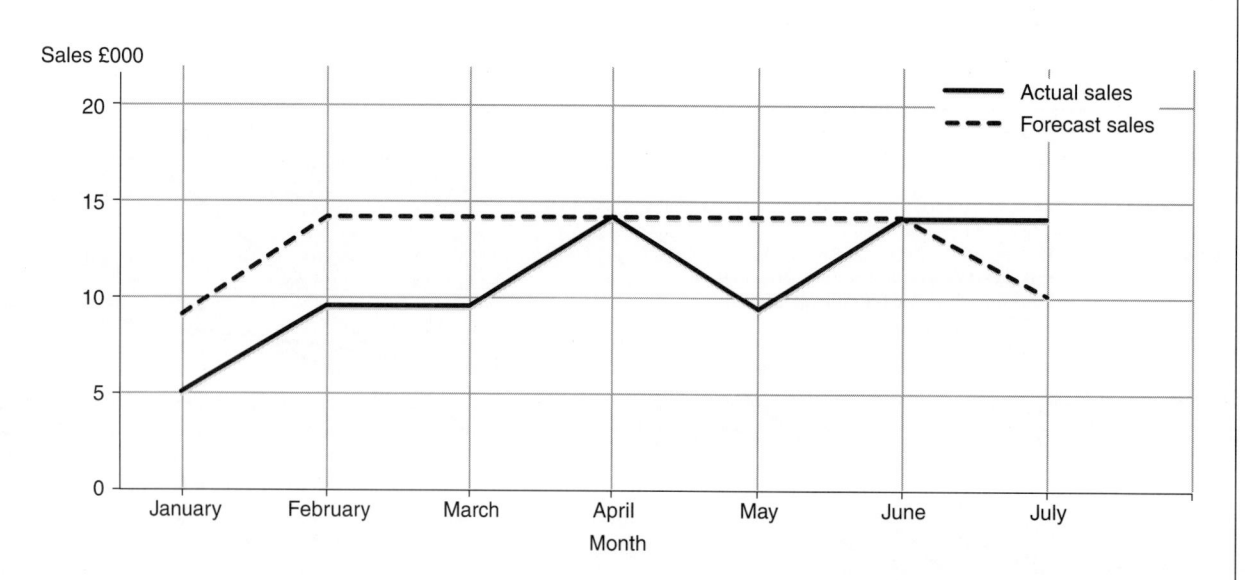

Sales Forecast influences:
- Cash flow forecast
- Profit (or loss) forecast
- Production plan i.e how many and what to make
- Number of people needed
- Expected stock levels

In January and February, for example, the actual sales are less than the forecasted sales. The firm will want to know why. For example, was it because the price was too high or the product was poor quality? In April the actual sales were the same as the forecast sales. In July the actual sales were higher than the forecasted level. The firm will want to know why. For example, was the advertising more effective than expected? did the product appeal to more people than expected?

38 Finance

Budgets, forecasts and cash flow continued

> Cash is a tangible money asset. It is shown in the current assets on the balance sheet. Cash flow statements show the flows of cash into and out of the business. Cash flow forecasts attempt to predict flows to highlight when cash might have to be borrowed or when it could be invested.

Cash flow forecast January - March

£000	January	February	March
Opening balance	20	(120)	100
Income	400	480	550
Expenditure	300	500	450
Closing balance	(120)	100	200

Opening balance: the amount of cash the firm has at the start of each month.
Income: cash inflows e.g. from sales.
Expenditure: cash outflows e.g. on wages, electricity and materials.

Closing balance: the amount of cash the firm has at the end of each month. The closing balance at the end of one month becomes the opening balance for the next month.

Improving cash flow

- chase debtors; get them to pay up **but** this may cause bad feelings
- insist customers pay cash **but** this may lead to a loss of business
- borrow (e.g. overdraft) **but** this will lead to interest payments
- sell assets (e.g. stocks, equipment) **but** may need these to produce

Cash flow forecasts may be incorrect because:

- debtors take longer to pay than expected
- sales are lower than expected
- costs are higher than expected e.g. interest rates increase.

Finance 39

Production

Types of production

- *Primary*: extractive industries, e.g. coal mining
- *Secondary*: manufacturing sector, e.g. carmakers
- *Tertiary*: services, e.g. travel agents

The UK has a small primary sector and has a growing tertiary sector.

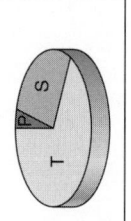

1993	%
Primary	3.9
Secondary	28.4
Tertiary	67.7

Methods of production

- **Job** one off or project production, e.g building a dam or a ship. Made to customer specifications; often labour intensive.
- **Batch** items are produced in 'batches', i.e they all undergo one operation before being moved onto the next operation, e.g baking bread.
- **Flow** continuous production process; each unit moves from one operation onto the next without waiting for a batch to be completed.
- **Mass** large scale production. Large numbers of identical products are made.

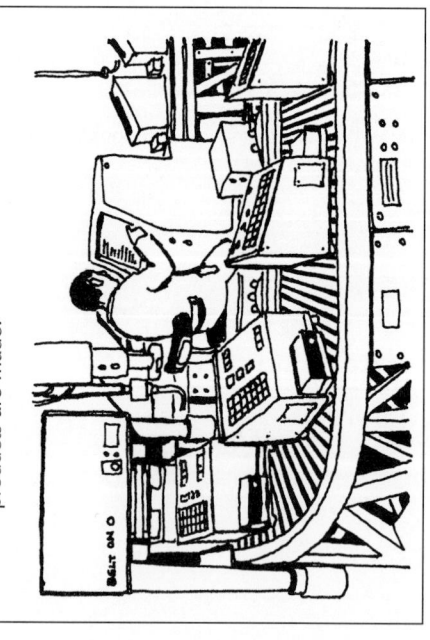

The production department

May involve:
- works manager or production manager - responsible for overall management of production.
- production engineering - how the product is made e.g. what procedures to use, what quality of materials to use, whether new equipment is needed
- production planning - deciding when the production will take place; what equipment to use and when; when to order material
- production control - checks that production plans are being followed, i.e. the right goods are being produced at the right time
- quality control - inspects the finished goods to make sure there are no defects.

Mass production

- usually involves high levels of capital compared to people, i.e. high levels of equipment. This will generally require a great deal of investment.
- to keep the cost per unit low, the firm must produce on a large scale. This type of production, therefore, is only suitable if there is a large market for the goods.

Mass production often involves the division of labour (also called 'specialisation')

Division of labour (specialisation)

The overall task is broken down into a series of relatively simple jobs. Individuals are given a fairly simple and repetitive job to do.

Advantages of division of labour

- individuals become better at the job because they are doing the same thing all the time
- people only have to be trained in one task

Problem of division of labour

- individuals become bored doing the same job all the time; this can lead to absenteeism, bad relations with management and a high labour turnover.

Productivity: $\frac{\text{OUTPUT}}{\text{INPUT}}$

Productivity can be increased by: training, higher motivation, more capital equipment

Subcontracting: using other producers to meet an order. Why ? To make use of specialist skills; because a firm is at full capacity and cannot meet the order; because it may be cheaper. Consider: the subcontractors' reliability, price and quality.

Idle time: occurs when the production process is not operational, e.g machines being broken down or waiting for materials to arrive or machines being retooled (reset) to produce a new product. Also called 'downtime'.

Research and development (R & D)

Studies new production methods and new products; develops and tests out new ideas. R & D may be undertaken by firms themselves or bought in from e.g universities. R & D represents an investment for the long term. It is a vital source of new ideas, innovation and competitive advantage. UK firms are often criticised for not undertaking enough research and development.

Work study:

examination of work to improve methods and establish suitable standards to assess performance.

Involves:

Method study - systematic process of recording and analysing existing and proposed methods of doing work to develop more effective and easier methods.

Work measurement - techniques to establish the time for a qualified worker to carry out a job at a given level of performance.

Technology

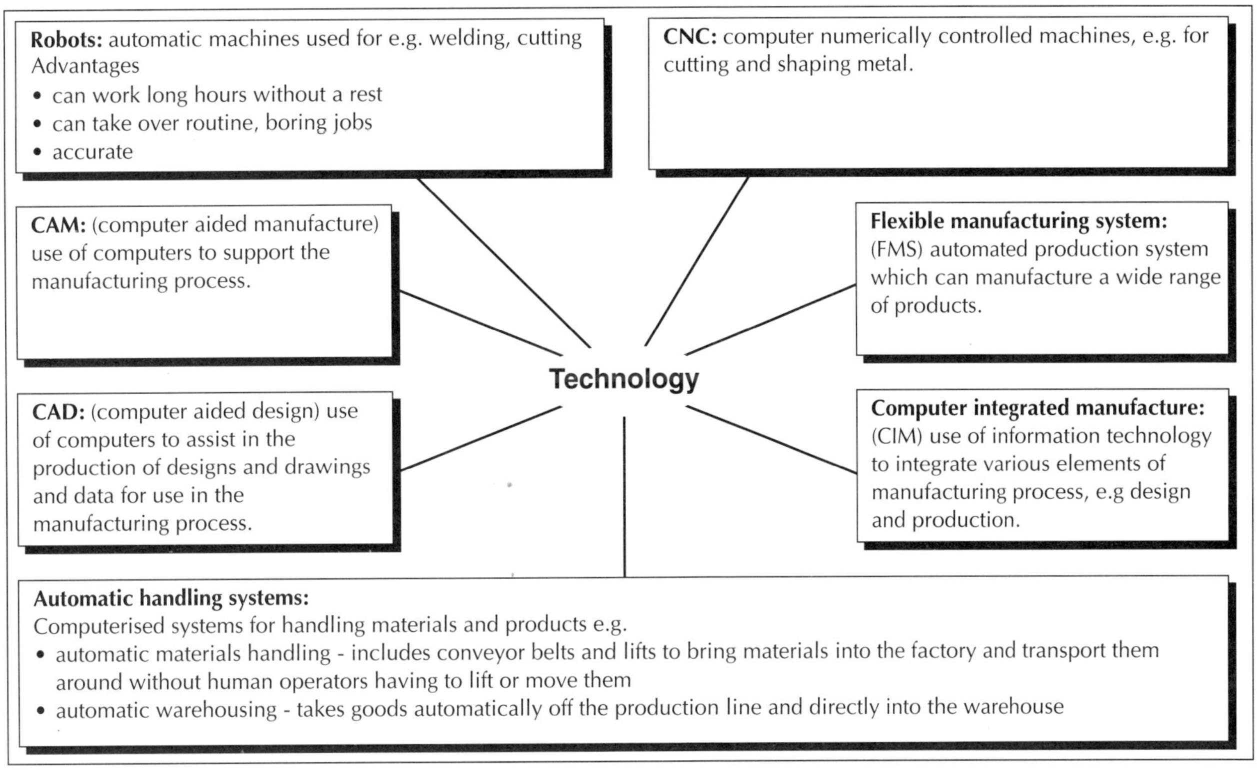

Robots: automatic machines used for e.g. welding, cutting
Advantages
- can work long hours without a rest
- can take over routine, boring jobs
- accurate

CNC: computer numerically controlled machines, e.g. for cutting and shaping metal.

CAM: (computer aided manufacture) use of computers to support the manufacturing process.

Flexible manufacturing system: (FMS) automated production system which can manufacture a wide range of products.

CAD: (computer aided design) use of computers to assist in the production of designs and drawings and data for use in the manufacturing process.

Computer integrated manufacture: (CIM) use of information technology to integrate various elements of manufacturing process, e.g design and production.

Automatic handling systems:
Computerised systems for handling materials and products e.g.
- automatic materials handling - includes conveyor belts and lifts to bring materials into the factory and transport them around without human operators having to lift or move them
- automatic warehousing - takes goods automatically off the production line and directly into the warehouse

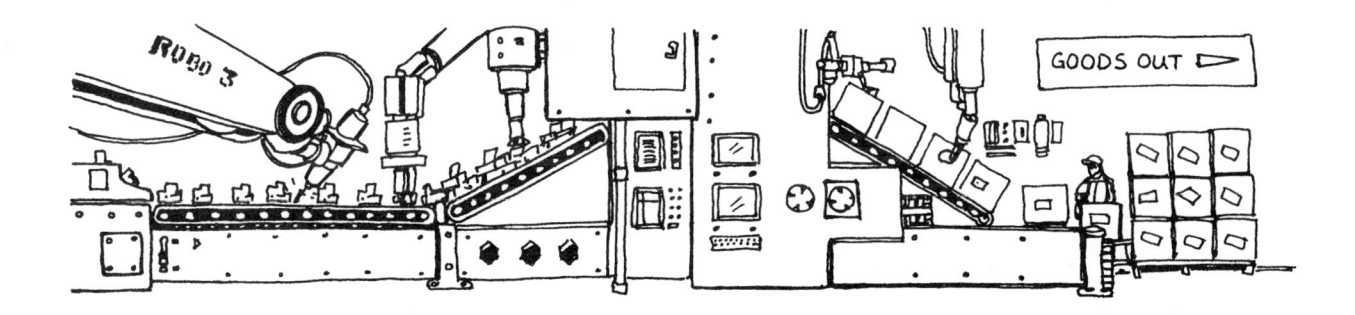

Technology
Technology is the way in which work is done, i.e. the equipment used and the way work is organised.

Improvements in technology lead to new products and processes.

The effects of technology include:
- new ways of working, e.g. more people working from home
- greater productivity/efficiency
- new products and markets, e.g. videocameras, microwaves
- more flexible manufacturing e.g computer aided design
- new skills needed
- loss of some jobs/creation of others
- improved communication, e.g. faxes, mobile phones
- shorter product life cycles
- quicker development times

When adopting technology firms should consider:
- initial cost
- employees' reaction
- training required
- expected benefits.

Just in time production: firms produce 'just in time' when goods or service are ordered. They do not hold stocks.

Advantages
- Minimises stock holding costs
- Money not tied up
- Focuses effort on quality as finished goods sent to customer immediately not left in stock

Disadvantages
- May not be able to meet sudden increase in demand
- Very reliant on suppliers and employees
- May lose bulk buying discounts
- Vulnerable to breakdowns

Production 41

Location

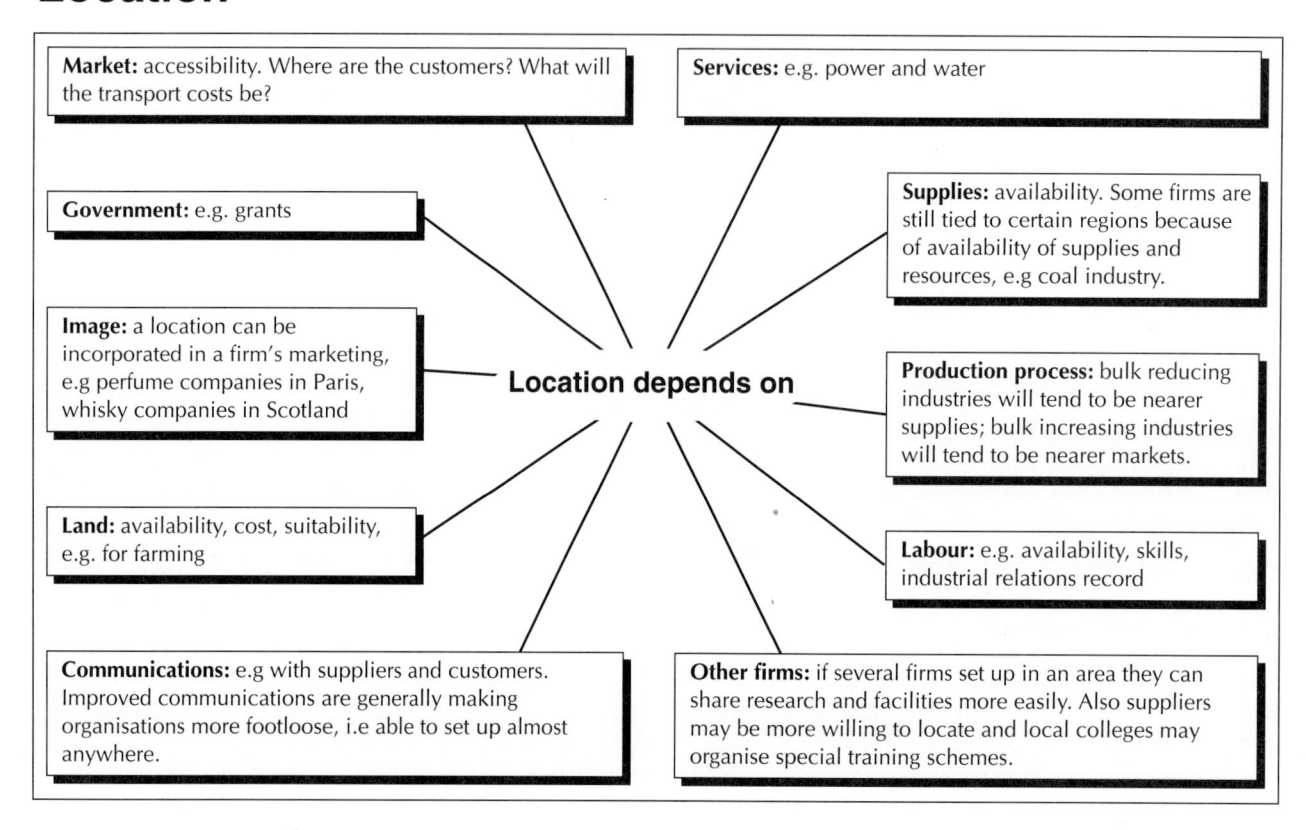

Market: accessibility. Where are the customers? What will the transport costs be?

Services: e.g. power and water

Government: e.g. grants

Supplies: availability. Some firms are still tied to certain regions because of availability of supplies and resources, e.g coal industry.

Image: a location can be incorporated in a firm's marketing, e.g perfume companies in Paris, whisky companies in Scotland

Location depends on

Production process: bulk reducing industries will tend to be nearer supplies; bulk increasing industries will tend to be nearer markets.

Land: availability, cost, suitability, e.g. for farming

Labour: e.g. availability, skills, industrial relations record

Communications: e.g with suppliers and customers. Improved communications are generally making organisations more footloose, i.e able to set up almost anywhere.

Other firms: if several firms set up in an area they can share research and facilities more easily. Also suppliers may be more willing to locate and local colleges may organise special training schemes.

Industrial inertia: firms stay in an area even if the original reason for locating there has gone.

Greenfield site: location which has no previous experience of a given type of industry.

Government assistance

Regional assistance is available in Development Areas and Intermediate Areas which are regions of severe economic decline.

- Selective Regional Assistance - discretionary grant towards capital and training costs.

- Regional Enterprise Grants - firms with fewer than 25 employees in Development Areas can gain investment grants or grants towards innovation or new process.

- Enterprise Zones - inner city areas; financial incentives offered to firms to locate here, e.g subsidised premises.

- Local Authority help - advice and grants for firms.

- Department of Trade and Industry - has an Investment in Britain Bureau to attract inward investment by overseas firms.

- European Union - also offers help for depressed areas via the European Regional Development Fund (money for infrastructure e.g roads) and the European Social Fund (money for training).

Purchasing and Stocks

Purchasing
The purchasing department is responsible for purchasing all the resources needed by the firm, e.g. materials, components, equipment.

The purchasing department must buy the right number of items at the right quality, at the right time for the right price, and have them delivered to the right place.

Stock control
The firm needs enough stock to keep producing and meet customer orders.

BUT

it is expensive to have stocks and so the firm does not want too many of them.

Cost of holding stocks:
- warehousing costs
- insurance and security costs
- stocks may depreciate
- opportunity costs - stocks tie up money which could be used elsewhere
- theft.

Stock control and information technology
Technology has made it easier to keep a record of the firm's stock. For example, when goods are scanned at the till in supermarkets, this can automatically deduct the item from the firm's records so it knows it has less items left.

Dangers of too little stock:
- Production may not be possible - may lead to down-time and idle labour
- May not be able to meet orders - lose customer loyalty; dissatisfied customers may tell others

The level of stocks held by a firm will depend on:
- the nature of the product, e.g. is the good perishable?
- suppliers, e.g. how often do they deliver? how reliable are they?
- the facilities available, e.g. warehouse space
- stockholding costs, e.g. insurance and security
- management policies, e.g. just in time production reduces stock levels.

Managing People

> The Personnel function is responsible for ensuring the firm has the right number of people with the right skills at the right time. This involves activities such as recruitment, selection, training, payment and promotion.
>
> People add value to the organisation by:
> - increasing productivity
> - improving quality
> - innovating
> - improving customer service

People can differentiate one organisation from another and are an important source of competitive advantage. Personnel management aims to enhance the contribution of individuals and groups towards the organisational objectives now and in the future.

This involves:
- attracting the right numbers of employees with the right skills and attitudes
- developing individuals to meet the challenges of their jobs now and in the future
- providing a safe and healthy environment in which to work
- enabling employees to contribute to the organisation
- developing an environment in which people are used to their full capacity and potential

Indicators of effective personnel management:

- low labour turnover: measured by

$$\frac{\text{number of employees leaving in given period}}{\text{average number employed}} \times 100$$

e.g. 12 leave out of 50 = $\frac{12}{50}$ × 100 = 24% labour turnover.

- high productivity (measured by output per worker)
- low wastage rates
- low scrap rates (i.e. relatively few products scrapped or reworked)
- good industrial relations
- cooperative workforce
- better customer service
- high quality production

Investors in People: Government award for firms which train and develop their employees.

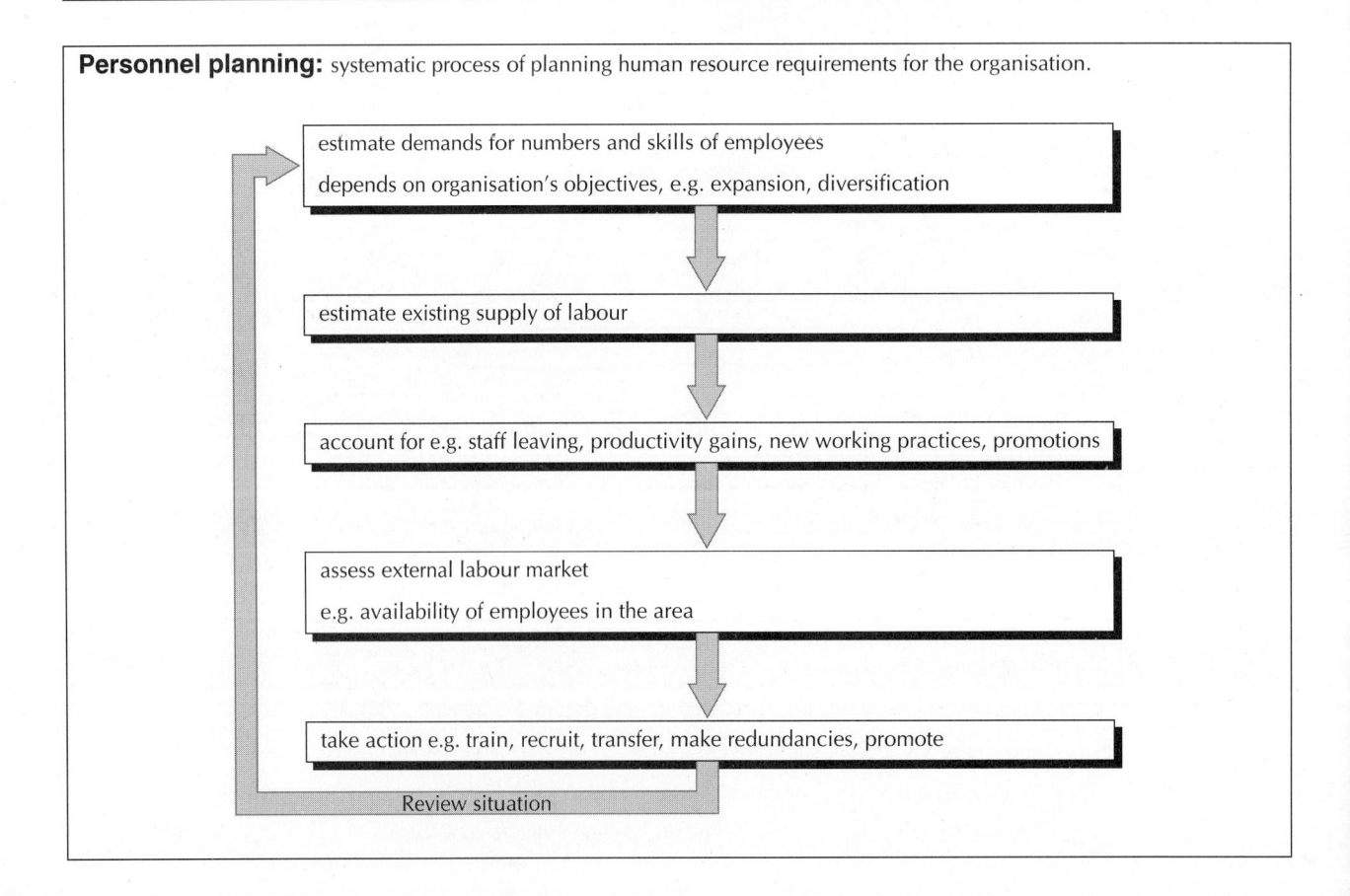

Personnel planning: systematic process of planning human resource requirements for the organisation.

- estimate demands for numbers and skills of employees
- depends on organisation's objectives, e.g. expansion, diversification

↓

- estimate existing supply of labour

↓

- account for e.g. staff leaving, productivity gains, new working practices, promotions

↓

- assess external labour market
- e.g. availability of employees in the area

↓

- take action e.g. train, recruit, transfer, make redundancies, promote

Review situation

44 People Management

Recruitment and selection

Hiring a new employee is an investment; it is important to get the right person for the right job. The right person will add value to an organisation; the wrong person can increase costs and reduce quality. Organisations can never be sure that they have selected the right person until he or she starts work, but an effective recruitment and selection process can reduce the risk.

Recruitment and selection process:

Job analysis:	process of examining the various elements of a job, e.g. its responsibilities, tasks, duties
Job evaluation:	assessment of the relative worth of a job; undertaken to ensure that the rewards of one job are fair compared to others in the organisation
Job description:	broad statement about a job, e.g. its job title, reporting relationships, duties, tasks
Person specification:	defines the requirements of the job holder e.g. experience, qualifications, disposition
Attract applicants: (see below)	e.g. advertise (internally or externally) contact job centres contact colleges/universities headhunt (i.e. recruit from other companies; also called poaching)
Applicants send: (see page 46)	Curriculum Vitae or fill in firm's application form or make direct contact
Selecting: (see page 46)	interview psychometric testing (personality test) aptitude testing (test skills e.g. word processing) intelligence testing medical - check health

Job advertisement

A job advert should contain the following information:

- job title
- the type of work involved
- the name of the firm
- where the job is based
- salary
- working conditions
- training (if appropriate)
- how the candidate should apply (e.g. send a curriculum vitae or telephone for an application form)

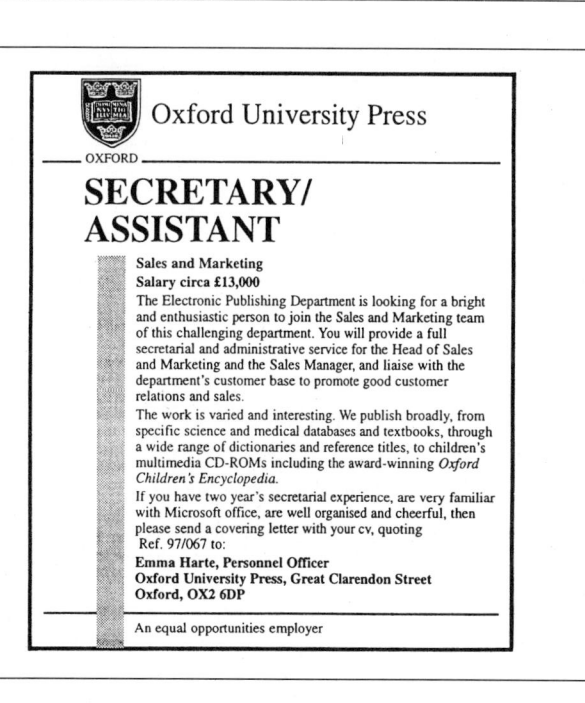

Oxford University Press

SECRETARY/ASSISTANT

Sales and Marketing
Salary circa £13,000

The Electronic Publishing Department is looking for a bright and enthusiastic person to join the Sales and Marketing team of this challenging department. You will provide a full secretarial and administrative service for the Head of Sales and Marketing and the Sales Manager, and liaise with the department's customer base to promote good customer relations and sales.

The work is varied and interesting. We publish broadly, from specific science and medical databases and textbooks, through a wide range of dictionaries and reference titles, to children's multimedia CD-ROMs including the award-winning *Oxford Children's Encyclopedia*.

If you have two year's secretarial experience, are very familiar with Microsoft office, are well organised and cheerful, then please send a covering letter with your cv, quoting Ref. 97/067 to:
Emma Harte, Personnel Officer
Oxford University Press, Great Clarendon Street
Oxford, OX2 6DP

An equal opportunities employer

People Management 45

Recruitment and selection continued

A Curriculum Vitae or CV provides information about a person, e.g. name, address, and qualifications. It is written by an applicant and sent to firms

Curriculum Vitae   Alison Watts

Address: 25 Farm Street
Upper Charlington, CH3 2DN

Telephone: 01297 734165

Date of birth: 14th November 1963

Work experience

1992 - present   Personnel Assistant to Sales Manager, Oxtem Ltd - small computer software company based in London. Work includes word processing, maintaining sales database, organising manager's diary. Experience of Windows 95, Word, Wordperfect and Access database.

1986 - 1992   Secretary at Brookers Publishing, Leicester. Working for Finance Director.

1984 - 1986   Office Assistant. General office duties.

Education

1985   Course in business and office skills, at West Oxpens College.

1984   St. Mary's College, Blackpool. O Levels English Literature B, English Language B, Maths B, French C, Geography C, History C.

Other qualifications

1985   RSA 3 Word Processing (Distinction).
Pitman Database (Merit), Spreadsheet (Distinction).

Interests

Classical Music and Jazz. I am grade 8 piano and play in a jazz band at weekends.

Interviewing

The interviewer should insure that:

- there are no interruptions
- he or she has read the applicant's details in advance
- he or she has prepared questions in advance
- the interview does not overrun (so the next applicant is not kept waiting)
- the interviewee is made to feel at ease and is given the chance to speak

The interview gives the firm the opportunity to assess the candidate's suitability for the job and gives the interviewee the chance to find out more about the firm and the job.

Advantages of recruiting:

Internally

- know the employee already
- employee knows organisation already
- may be quicker
- may be cheaper
- motivates employees

Externally

- more choice
- can benefit from the experience of employees who have worked for other firms.

When recruiting consider:

- how much time is available before vacancy has to be filled?
- how much money should be/can be spent?
- what is most effective means of attracting applicants, e.g. unlikely to advertise nationally for a very junior post
- what is the state of the labour market?
- what is an appropriate reward package?

Assessing the effectiveness of the recruitment and selection process:

- Ratios, e.g. number of applicants : number manager felt were suitable to be interviewed
- Performance in the job once recruited
- Cost
- Time taken
- Retention rates, i.e. how long do people stay once they have been recruited?

46 People Management

Employment

Offering the job: employees are entitled to a written contract of employment within 13 weeks of starting work. It includes: job title, rate of pay and method of pay, normal hours of work, holiday arrangements, sick pay and pension arrangements, disciplinary and grievance procedures, and the length of notice due to and from the employee.

Training

Induction training: introduces employees to their job and the organisation as a whole, e.g history, mission, rules

On the job training: employees learn whilst undertaking the job

Off the job training: employees trained away from the actual job; may be within firm or at outside college.

Training and Enterprise Councils: local organisations responsible for organising and administering training in their regions.

NVQs: National Vocational Qualifications; qualifications employees can gain at work.

GNVQs: General National Vocational Qualifications; these are studied at school or college and are more work related qualifications than A levels.

Government training schemes: have included Youth Training (for 16 year old school leavers to receive on the job training) and Employment Training for the long term unemployed

The value of training:
- increases employees' skills in their present jobs
- prepares employees for change
- increases the organisations flexibility
- motivates employees
- can reduce mistakes and improve profits.

Appraisal: assessing an employee's performance in his or her job. This should be an ongoing process but some organisations also have a formal appraisal process. Used to identify training needs.

Policies and procedures

Discipline procedure: process by which employees are disciplined, e.g verbal warning, written warning, final written warning and dismissal.

Grievance procedure: process by which employees can complain about the way in which they are treated

Equal opportunities policy: provides employees with the same opportunities regardless of race or colour or gender, i.e. does not discriminate.

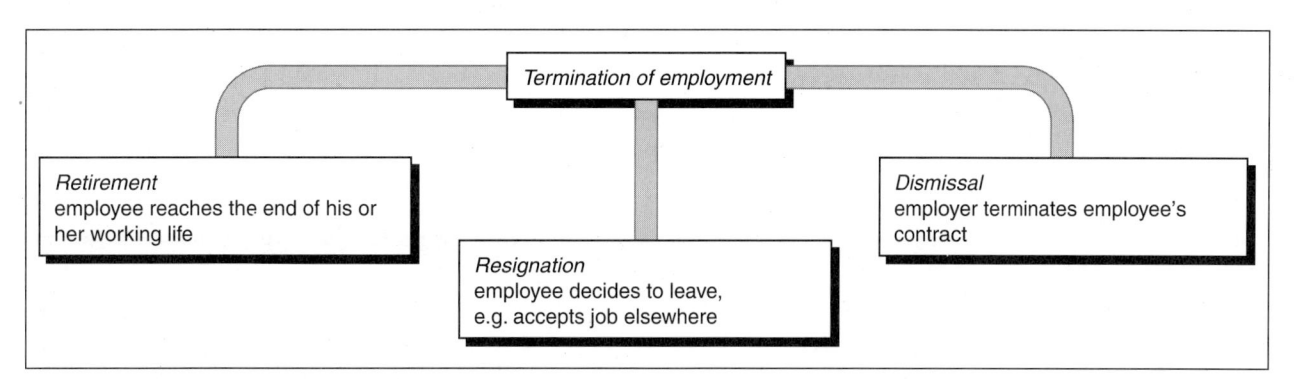

Termination of employment

Retirement — employee reaches the end of his or her working life

Resignation — employee decides to leave, e.g. accepts job elsewhere

Dismissal — employer terminates employee's contract

Dismissal

Fair dismissal: termination of an individual's employment contract for a fair reason according to the law.

Fair reasons include:
- illegality, e.g. employee lied about qualifications
- incapability - employee is incapable of doing the work
- job no longer exists (redundancy)
- any other substantial reason, e.g. physical assault

Unfair dismissal: the reason for the termination of employment is regarded as unfair in law, e.g. cannot dismiss someone for being a member of a union or for being pregnant.

Summary dismissal: employee dismissed on the spot without a further warning. Only occurs when there has been a severe breach of the organisation's rules (called 'gross misconduct').

Industrial tribunal

If employees feel they have been unfairly dismissed or discriminated against, they can appeal to an *industrial tribunal;* this is an industrial court which judges whether or not the employer behaved fairly.

Employment continued

Redundancy: an employee is made redundant because of the closure of all or part of the business. An employee who has worked full time for the organisation for more than two years or part time for five years is entitled to statutory redundancy pay. (Full time is defined as more than 16 hours per week). Firms may pay more than the legal requirement.

Outplacement services: are provided by some firms to help employees find alternative employment. May involve information, advice and the provision of various facilities (e.g. reference books, newspapers, word processors).

Issues with redundancy

Employers must consider:

- which jobs to cut
- how to select employees
- the amount of notice to be given
- the degree of consultation
- redundancy payments

Voluntary redundancy: occurs when individuals are willing to be made redundant (i.e. they volunteer for it).

Employment patterns

Changes in the UK labour market in the 1980s and 1990s:

- older population
- less younger people entering workforce
- more women workers
- more part time workers
- more jobs in the service sector
- more flexible working patterns

Flexible working patterns:

- flexitime: employees have some freedom over what hours they work
- temporary workers: employees work for a few days or a few weeks at a time
- multi-skilling: employees trained in a variety of tasks
- homeworking: working at home, e.g. telecommuting - working via computer
- part time jobs: employees work a few hours each week
- job sharing: two or more people share job, e.g. one works mornings, another works afternoons.

Flexible working patterns

- allow firms to increase or decrease their output more easily. This means that firms can match supply to demand more effectively
- allow individuals to develop work patterns which suit their own lifestyles e.g. part time work whilst raising children.

Employment type	1985 %	1995 %	2005 (estimated) %
Permanent	84	82	79
Part time	21	24	25
Self employed	11	13	13.5
Temporary	5	6	8

Source: Business Strategies

Unions

Represent, protect, inform, and provide services for employees on a factory, local, and national level.

Types of unions:
- craft - for employees with a particular skill, e.g. electricians AEEU
- industry - for employees in particular industry, e.g. coalminers NUM
- general - broad union for wide range of employees usually unskilled or semi-skilled, e.g. TGWU
- white collar - for clerical, professional or managerial staff, e.g. NUT (teachers)
- staff associations for employees in a particular organisation, e.g. Marks and Spencer

Union recognition: occurs when an employer agrees to bargain with a union over, e.g. wages. Employers do not have to recognise unions but employees cannot be prevented from joining a union.

Industrial relations: the state of the relationship between employer, unions and employees. Also called 'employment relations'

Benefits of unions

To employers
- channel of communication
- can highlight human resource implications of any action
- provide ideas/ information

To employees
- provide power
- provide advice
- provide services, e.g. legal advice if dismissed
- provide protection

Employees' views of what a trade union should try to do:

	1994 %
protect existing jobs	37
improve working conditions	20
improve pay	15
have more say over management's long term plans	14
have more say over how work is done day to day	5
reduce pay differences at the workplace	4
work for equal opportunities for women	2

Source: British Attitudes Survey, Social and Community Planning Research

Consultation with unions
managers ask union representatives for their opinions; managers make final decision

v.

Bargaining with unions
managers negotiate with unions; final decision depends on negotiation

Collective bargaining: union representative negotiates on behalf of a group of employees. Employees have more power as they are bargaining as a group rather than individually.

Forms of industrial action:
- overtime ban - can make it difficult for a firm to meet its orders
- sit in - employees occupy premises
- go slow - employees work at a slow rate
- work to rule - employees stick to their contracts absolutely; this often slows up their work considerably.
- strikes - employees refuse to work. To be official employees must have a secret ballot and gain a majority.

Determinants of union strength:
- the percentage of employees who are members (called the 'unionisation rate' or 'union density')
- the degree of public support
- management attitude
- legal environment
- the ability of management to find alternative labour
- union and management resources

People Management 49

Unions continued

Employment Laws

Major changes affecting unions include: 1980, 1982, 1988, 1989, 1990 Employment Acts, 1984 Trade Union Act, Trade Union Reform and Employment Rights Act 1993.

The effects of changes in the laws in the 1980s and 1990s include:

- a union must have a secret ballot before it can have an official strike
- a union is liable for damages if a strike is unofficial
- a code of practice recommends a maximum of 6 official pickets (employees who protest outside a factory to persuade others not to go to work)
- secondary picketing is illegal (i.e. workers can only protest at the place of work where the original dispute occurred; cannot try to influence employees at other places, e.g. suppliers or distributors)
- senior union officials must be elected at least every five years
- unions must provides at least seven days notice of official industrial action

Union membership has declined since the late 1970s. A major reason is the growth of employment in sectors where unions are not traditionally very strong, e.g. part timers, the service sector, south east, and women workers.

Trade union membership, 1900–1993 (UK)

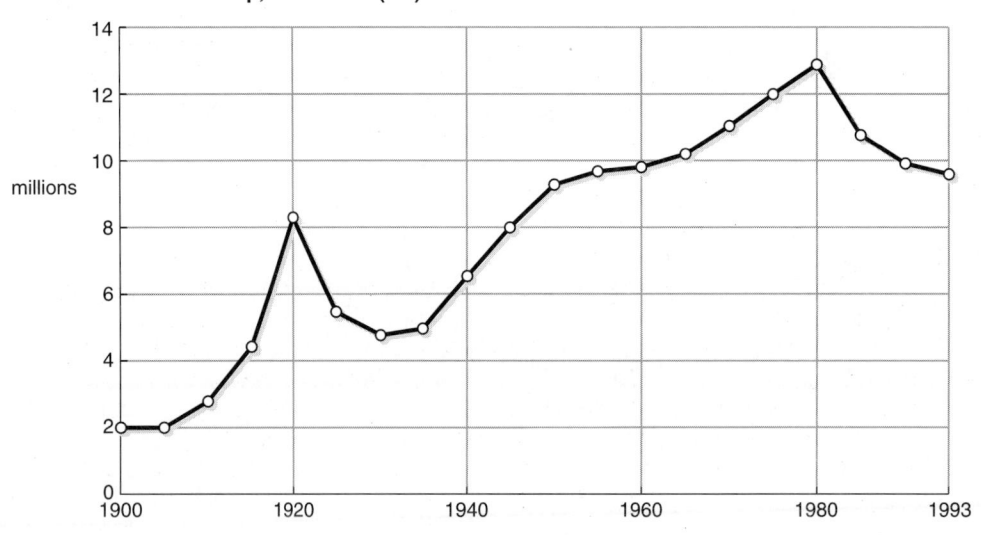

Organisations

ACAS: Advisory Conciliation and Arbitration Service. Independent body set up by the Government in the 1970s. Provides advice to employers and employees on industrial relations. If asked it will attempt to bring the two sides in a dispute together (conciliate). If this does not work, ACAS (if asked by both sides) will solve the dispute by making the decision itself (arbitration).

TUC: Trades Union Congress. Represents most unions at national and international level; attempts to influence public opinion and Government.

CBI: Confederation of British Industry. Represents firms in private sector; attempts to influence public opinion and the government; attempts to promote image of industry; provides information on industry for members.

Employers' associations: represent employers' views and interests in a particular industry, e.g. EEF (Engineering Employees' Federation).

Motivation in theory

Motivation is the extent to which an individual makes an effort to do something

Key elements of motivation

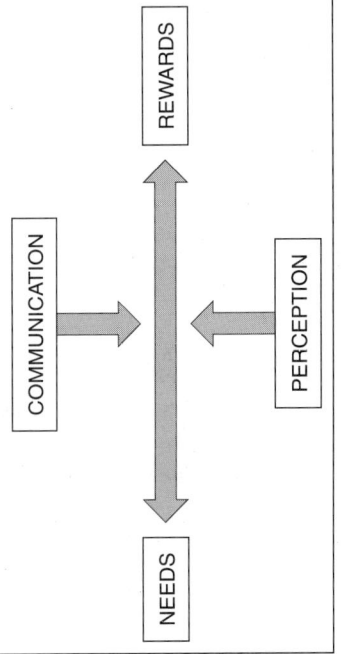

```
         COMMUNICATION
              ↓
     NEEDS ←→ REWARDS
              ↑
          PERCEPTION
```

To motivate:
- appropriate rewards must be offered
- individuals must know how to achieve these rewards
- individuals must believe they are capable of achieving them
- individuals must perceive the rewards are fair

Motivated employees are likely:
- to be more productive
- to have better attendance rates
- to be more co-operative and open to change
- to produce better quality work.

Herzberg's Two Factor Theory:
Hygiene factors: prevent dissatisfaction if they are present but do not actually satisfy e.g. acceptable working conditions, rules, basic pay

Motivators: factors at work which actually satisfy if they are present, e.g. responsibility, recognition, the chance of promotion

hygiene factors → motivators

Why do people work?
- to earn money to buy goods and services
- to face challenges, e.g. to make decisions, to lead a team of people
- to work with others

Job satisfaction
This depends on
- the amount of pay: How much is it? How much is it compared to other people? How much is it compared to how hard the person works? Are there bonuses for good performance?
- the fringe benefits
- the job itself - Is it challenging? Does it allow you to take responsibility?
- the conditions of work - How many hours does the job involve? Are the working conditions pleasant?
- the opportunities for more responsibility and promotion
- the people you work with - Are they easy to get along with? Are they interesting?
- the management - Do they treat the staff with respect? Are they fair? Are they encouraging? Do they praise employees when they have done good work?

Maslow
Maslow's hierarchy of needs:

- self actualisation needs - need to achieve for oneself
- esteem/ego needs - need to be recognised, acknowledged
- social needs - need to belong, to be loved
- security needs - need to feel safe
- physiological needs - need to survive, to eat and drink

According to Maslow:
Individuals will be motivated if the reward satisfies an unfulfilled need. Once satisfied a need no longer motivates; individuals will want the next level of need satisfied.

WORKER OF THE YEAR 1997

People Management 51

Motivation in practice

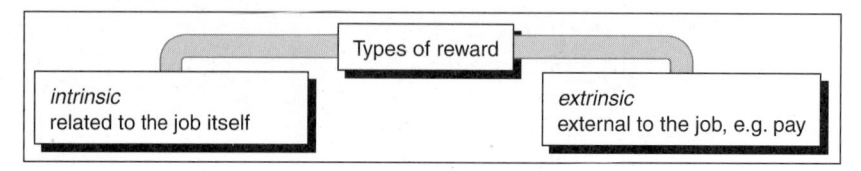

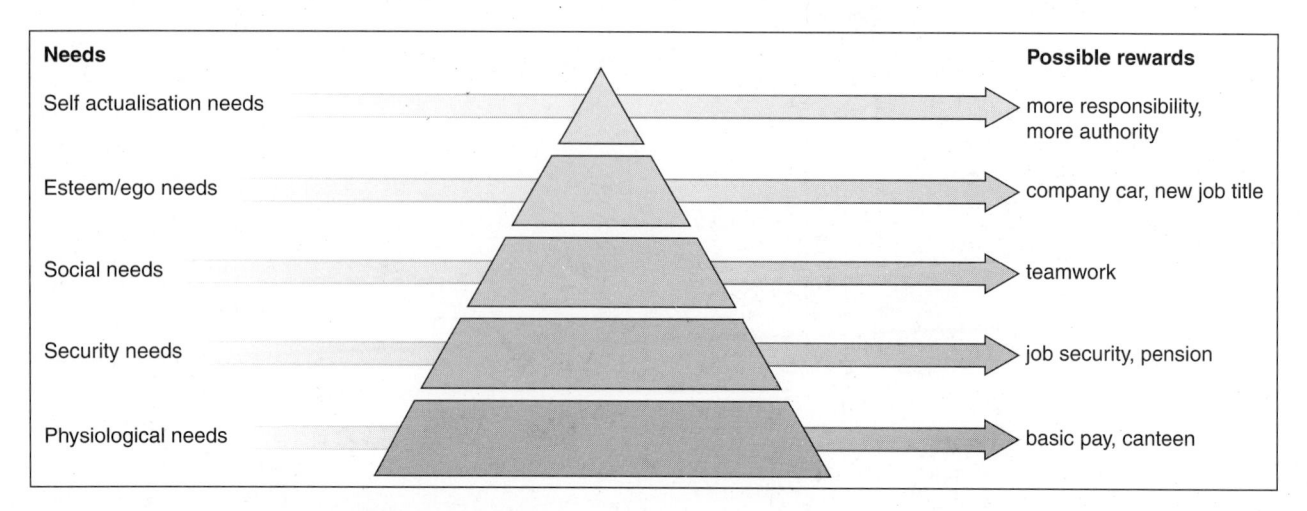

Types of reward

intrinsic — related to the job itself

extrinsic — external to the job, e.g. pay

Needs	Possible rewards
Self actualisation needs	more responsibility, more authority
Esteem/ego needs	company car, new job title
Social needs	teamwork
Security needs	job security, pension
Physiological needs	basic pay, canteen

Motivating jobs should:

- provide variety
- allow individuals some responsibility
- provide employees with feedback
- provide employees with a complete unit of work, not just a small part of a job
- have a sense of purpose

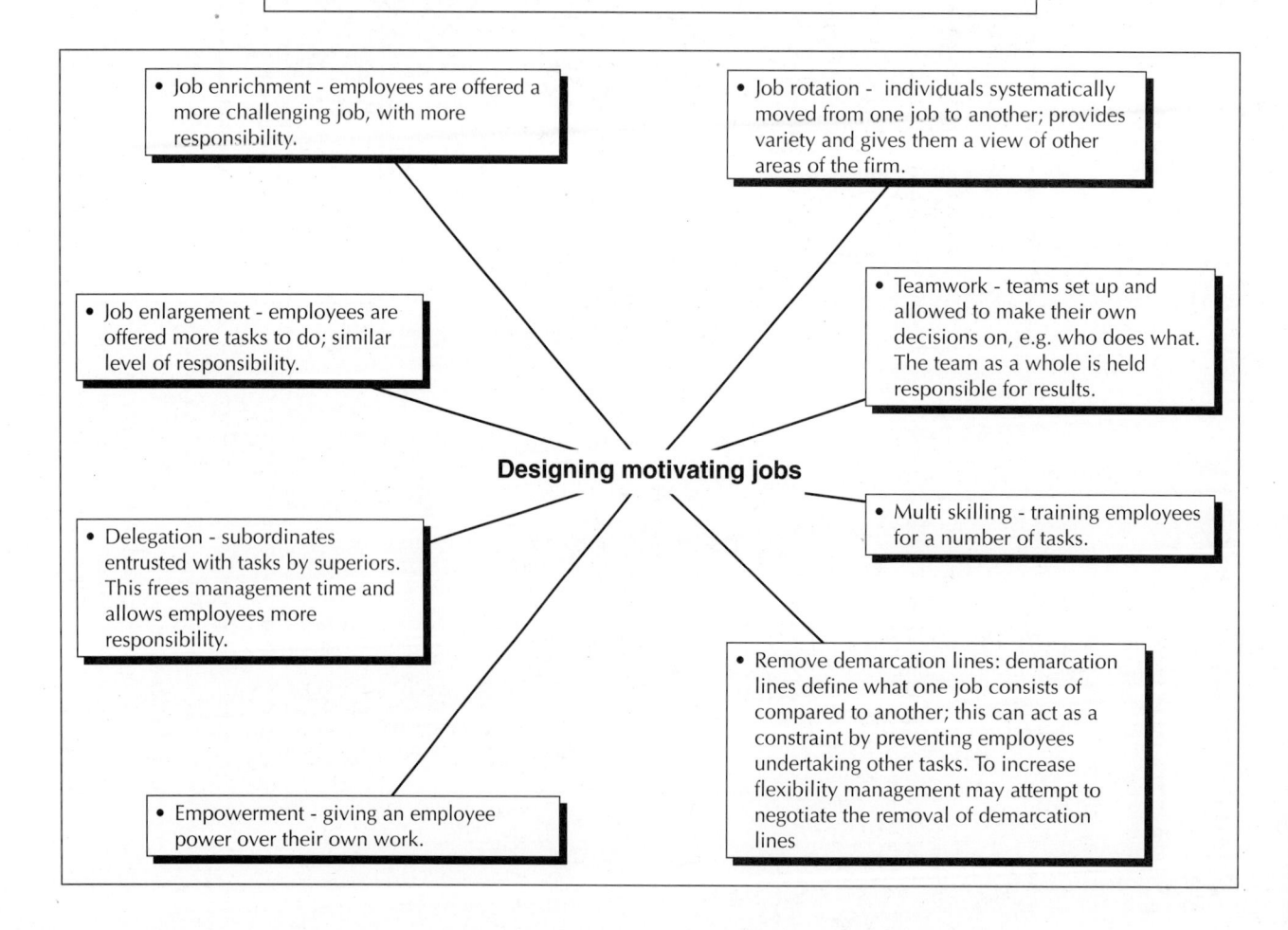

Designing motivating jobs

- **Job enrichment** - employees are offered a more challenging job, with more responsibility.
- **Job rotation** - individuals systematically moved from one job to another; provides variety and gives them a view of other areas of the firm.
- **Job enlargement** - employees are offered more tasks to do; similar level of responsibility.
- **Teamwork** - teams set up and allowed to make their own decisions on, e.g. who does what. The team as a whole is held responsible for results.
- **Delegation** - subordinates entrusted with tasks by superiors. This frees management time and allows employees more responsibility.
- **Multi skilling** - training employees for a number of tasks.
- **Empowerment** - giving an employee power over their own work.
- **Remove demarcation lines:** demarcation lines define what one job consists of compared to another; this can act as a constraint by preventing employees undertaking other tasks. To increase flexibility management may attempt to negotiate the removal of demarcation lines

52 People Management

Reward systems

Payment systems:

- time rate: pay by the hour, e.g. shop assistants. This system relies on individuals using their time productively. If employees work more than the agreed number of hours they may be paid 'over-time' at a higher rate.

- performance related pay: pay on performance, e.g. piece rate (employees paid for each unit of output). Should be motivating but quality can suffer as individuals rush to complete work. 'Commission' occurs when individuals are paid a percentage of sales. Does not work if it is difficult to measure output e.g. receptionist.

- salary: set amount per year; paid monthly (whereas wages are paid weekly). Shows that employers trust employees to use their time effectively.

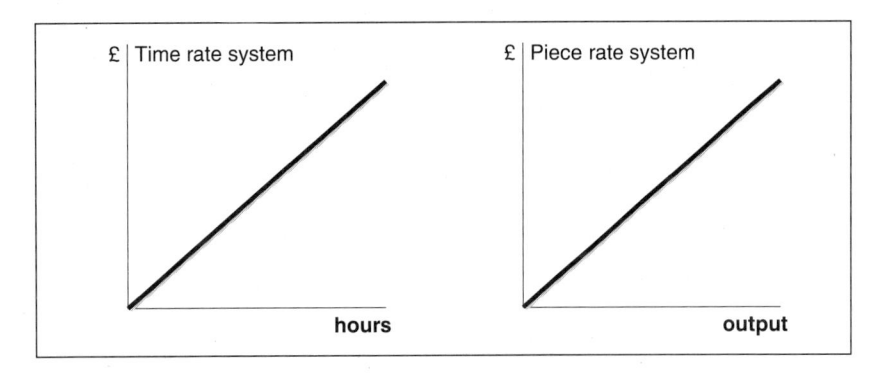

[Graph: Time rate system — £ vs hours, linear]
[Graph: Piece rate system — £ vs output, linear]

Incentive schemes:

- profit sharing - individuals receive a proportion of company profits
- bonus scheme - additional payments if set targets are exceeded

Fringe benefits:

- company car
- contributions to pension schemes
- contributions to health schemes
- subsidised canteen
- relocation allowance if moved an employee is from one area to another
- lower prices for company goods and services

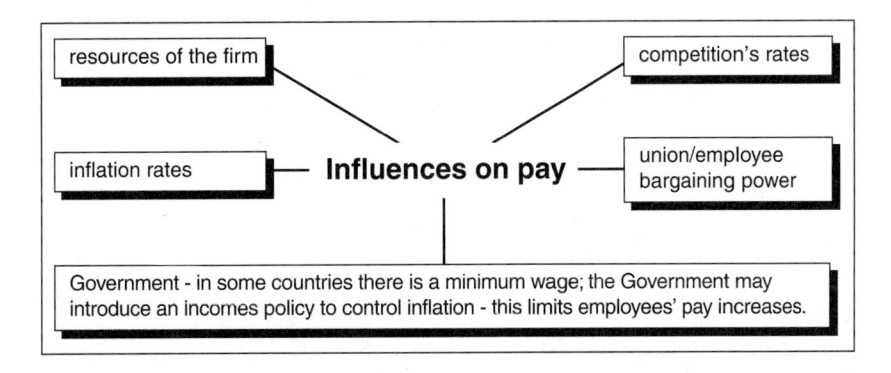

Influences on pay
- resources of the firm
- competition's rates
- inflation rates
- union/employee bargaining power
- Government - in some countries there is a minimum wage; the Government may introduce an incomes policy to control inflation - this limits employees' pay increases.

Successful reward systems

Successful reward systems will:

- attract and retain sufficient numbers of suitable employees
- reward employees for effort, experience, loyalty and achievement

People Management

Pay and pay slips

Gross pay: the amount earned before any deductions are made
Net pay (or take home pay): the amount received by employees after deductions are made from gross pay.

Deductions from pay:

Income tax - usually deducted from gross pay before the person is actually paid any money. This system is called Pay As You Earn (PAYE).

National Insurance Contributions (NI)
These contributions are mainly used for the state pension when employees retire.

Union membership
If an employee is a member of a union he or she may arrange for the membership fee to be directly deducted monthly from gross pay.

Company Pension
An employee may belong to the company pension scheme. Contributions are paid into a fund; this money is invested to pay out a pension when he or she retires.

Allowances
Individuals are entitled to earn certain amounts of money before paying taxes. These are called tax free allowances.

Outgoings
Employees can claim some outgoings against tax to reduce their tax bill, e.g. membership fees for a professional organisation and travel costs.

Business expenses
Some business expenses also qualify for tax relief, e.g. self employed can get tax relief on their rent, advertising and telephone bills.

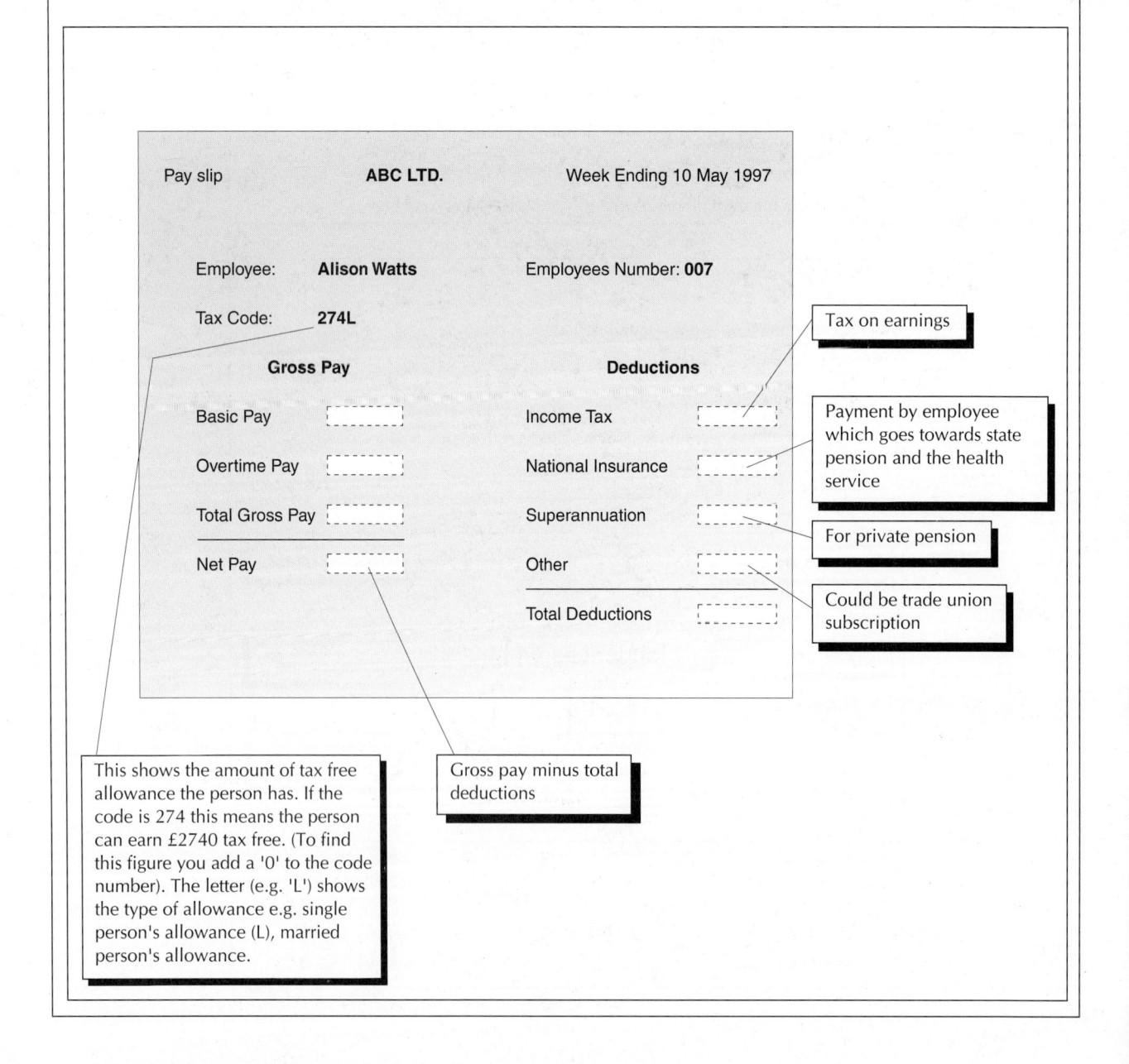

Pay slip   **ABC LTD.**   Week Ending 10 May 1997

Employee: **Alison Watts**   Employees Number: **007**

Tax Code: **274L**

Gross Pay		Deductions	
Basic Pay		Income Tax	
Overtime Pay		National Insurance	
Total Gross Pay		Superannuation	
Net Pay		Other	
		Total Deductions	

- Tax on earnings
- Payment by employee which goes towards state pension and the health service
- For private pension
- Could be trade union subscription

This shows the amount of tax free allowance the person has. If the code is 274 this means the person can earn £2740 tax free. (To find this figure you add a '0' to the code number). The letter (e.g. 'L') shows the type of allowance e.g. single person's allowance (L), married person's allowance.

Gross pay minus total deductions

54 People Management

Internal organisation of business

Organisational chart: represents the organisational structure. It shows reporting relationships but does not show the authority of each position.

Chain of command: line of command from top to bottom of organisation. Vertical line of authority.

Span of control: number of subordinates directly responsible to a superior. A narrow span enables managers to keep control and reduces risk. A wide span develops subordinates and enables them to have greater freedom; allows for less levels of management.

Size of span depends on: ability of subordinates to complete the task, whether the task is simple or complex; the ability of the superior to oversee employees; and the quality of communication.

Hierarchy: level of responsibility

Authority: legitimate power.

Responsibility: obligation to complete a task effectively.

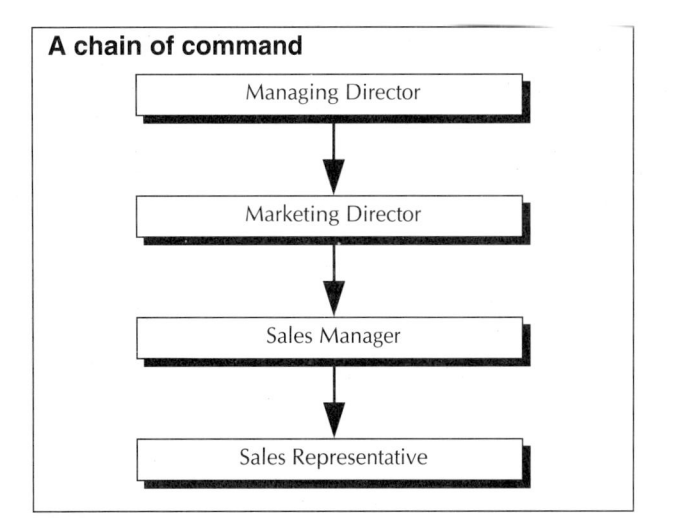

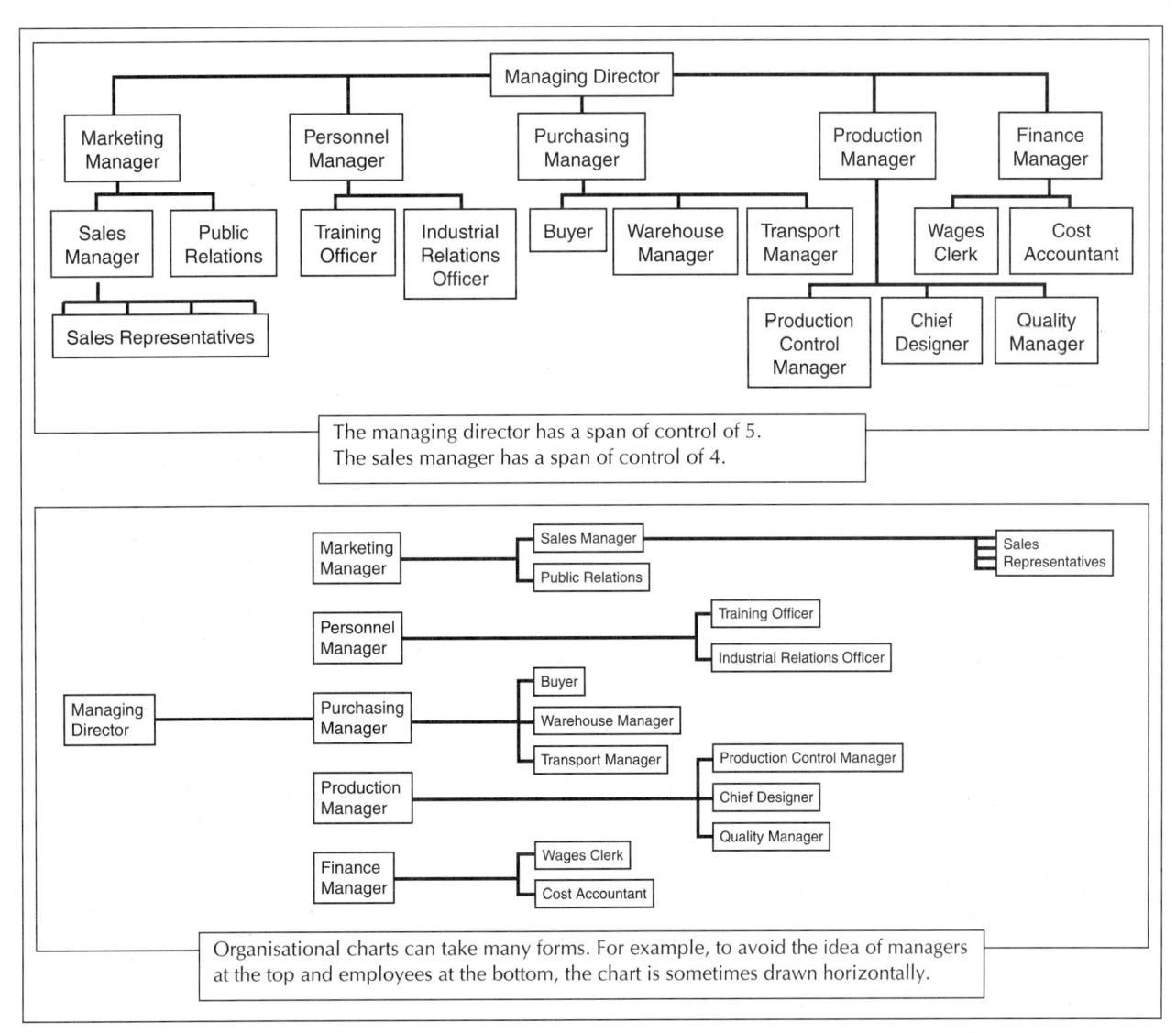

A chain of command

Managing Director → Marketing Director → Sales Manager → Sales Representative

The managing director has a span of control of 5.
The sales manager has a span of control of 4.

Organisational charts can take many forms. For example, to avoid the idea of managers at the top and employees at the bottom, the chart is sometimes drawn horizontally.

Delayering

A trend in the 1980s and 1990s is 'delayering'. This involves reducing the levels of hierarchy and wider spans; this increases the responsibility of employers and reduces the need for middle management.

People Management

Internal organisation of business continued

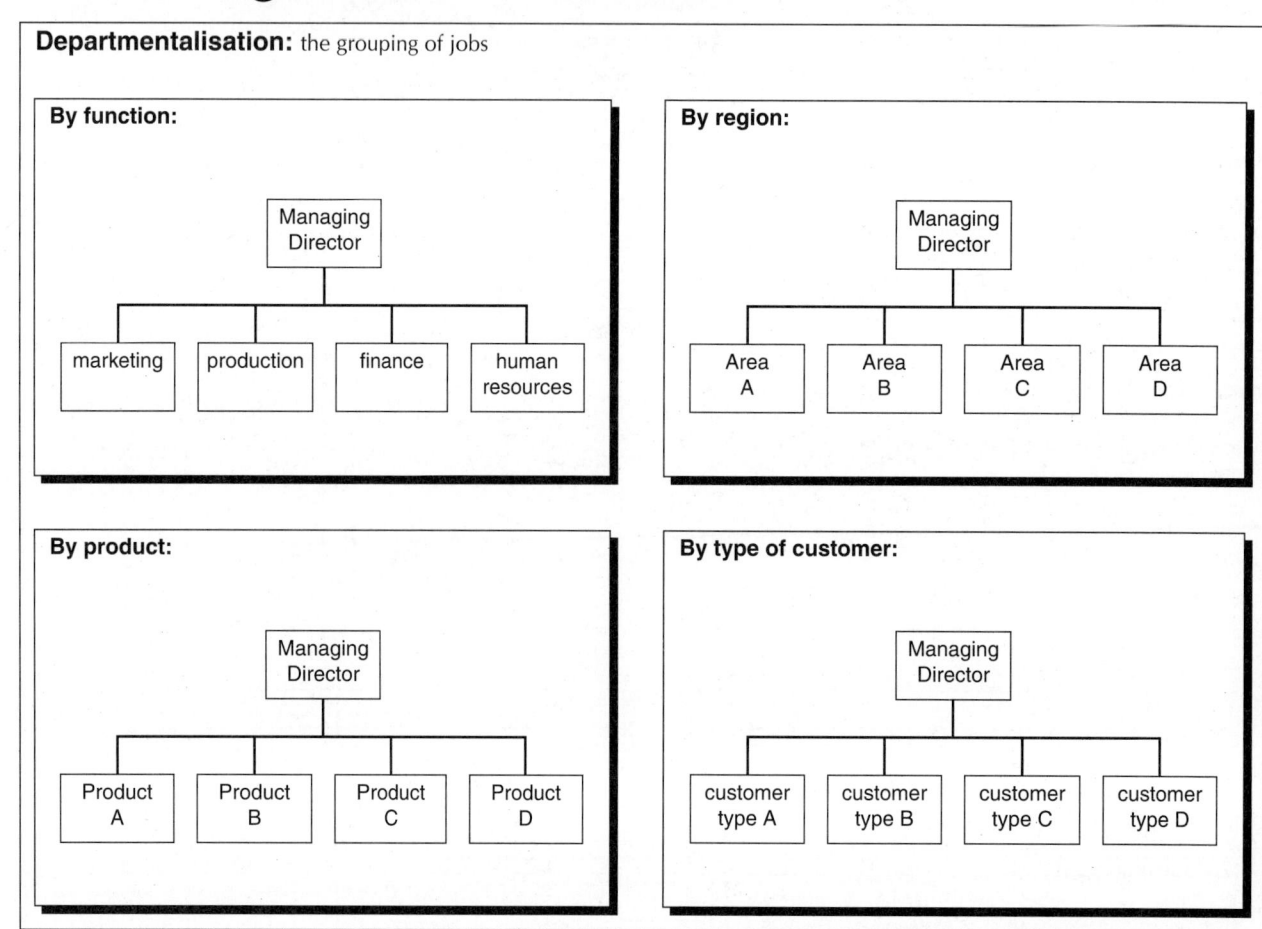

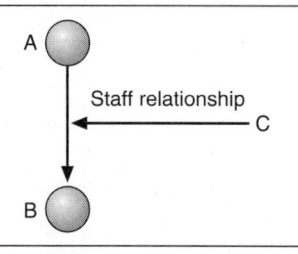

Departmentalisation: the grouping of jobs

By function:

```
        Managing
        Director
    ┌──────┼──────┬──────┐
marketing production finance human
                              resources
```

By region:

```
        Managing
        Director
    ┌──────┼──────┬──────┐
  Area   Area   Area   Area
   A      B      C      D
```

By product:

```
        Managing
        Director
    ┌──────┼──────┬──────┐
 Product Product Product Product
   A       B       C       D
```

By type of customer:

```
          Managing
          Director
    ┌──────┼──────┬──────┐
customer customer customer customer
 type A   type B   type C   type D
```

```
   A ●
     │
     │  Staff relationship
     │◄──────────── C
     ▼
   B ●
```

Line relationship: A to B; direct authority relationship, e.g. production manager to production supervisor

Staff relationship: C to A; advisory relationship which has no direct authority over the line; an expert or specialist who provides information to the line manager, e.g. market research or human resources function.

'Staff' sometimes get frustrated because they can only advise; line may not pay any attention.

Centralisation: main decisions made by senior management; little authority is passed down the organisation. Advantages: decisions made by experienced people with overview. Ensures policies are consistent throughout the organisation.

Decentralisation: extent to which authority passed down the organisation. Advantage: enables divisions or departments to react quickly to their market conditions.

The trend in the 1980s and 1990s is to decentralise to provide greater flexibility.

If the internal organisation is wrong:

- motivation may decrease - people do not know what is happening or why
- decision making can be slow
- lack of coordination
- costs can rise
- failure to share ideas

56 People Management

Government

'Government' includes central and local government:

Central government

Provides services such as defence and the National Health Service. Some activities are run by government departments

Departments include:

The Treasury - responsible for economic strategy

Departments: of Social Security (provides benefits), of Trade and Industry, of Transport

QUANGOs (specialised bodies with specific responsibilities, e.g. Sports Council and Arts Council)

Central government raises money from taxation and selling government bonds (IOUs) ie. borrowing

Local authorities
include county councils and district councils. They provide services in their local areas such as:

- education and recreation, e.g. libraries and sports centres
- housing, e.g. council houses
- environmental services, e.g. refuse collection
- road maintenance
- social services, e.g. care for the elderly

Local authorities are funded by central government and the council tax. They also get revenue from services such as swimming pools and leisure centres

The Government

Central government can influence:

- the firm's location (through regional policy)
- the firm's costs and prices (through subsidies and taxation)
- the firm's responsibilities to its workforce (through employment legislation)
- the firm's responsibilities to consumers (through consumer legislation)
- the firm's ability to trade abroad and international competitiveness (through treaties and the exchange rate)

Local authorities can influence a firm through planning permission. Before a firm can expand its factory or alter its premises, it needs planning permission from the local authority. The authority will also be responsible for enforcing laws such as the Health and Safety at Work Act.

Firms and households also pay rates (a form of tax) to the local authorities. Other taxes include:
- national insurance - this is a certain percentage of an individual's pay
- value added tax - paid when you buy most goods and services
- rates - paid on property
- excise duties - paid on certain goods such as alcohol
- corporation tax - paid by firms as a percentage of their profits

The Government can help firms by
- providing information and advice e.g. through Training and Enterprise Councils
- providing grants for companies who set up in certain areas (regional assistance)
- providing help for small firms or people wanting to set up In business. For example, Enterprise Allowances are offered to people who are unemployed and want to start in business
- providing help for exporters, e.g. through the British Overseas Trade Board
- training - the Government provides various training schemes to help people have the skills to work and set up in business.

Regional policy

Assistance is available to firms which set up in particular areas. The Government gives grants and subsidies to encourage firms to set up in areas of high unemployment. Grants include the Regional Enterprise Grant. The Government has also created the Enterprise Zones which are areas free of many of the regulations that businesses normally have to follow. This makes it easier and more attractive to set up there.

Government continued

The objectives of Government include:
- growth   i.e. increase the income of the economy
- stable prices   i.e control inflation
- a healthy balance of payments   i.e. increase exports
- full employment   i.e. reduce unemployment

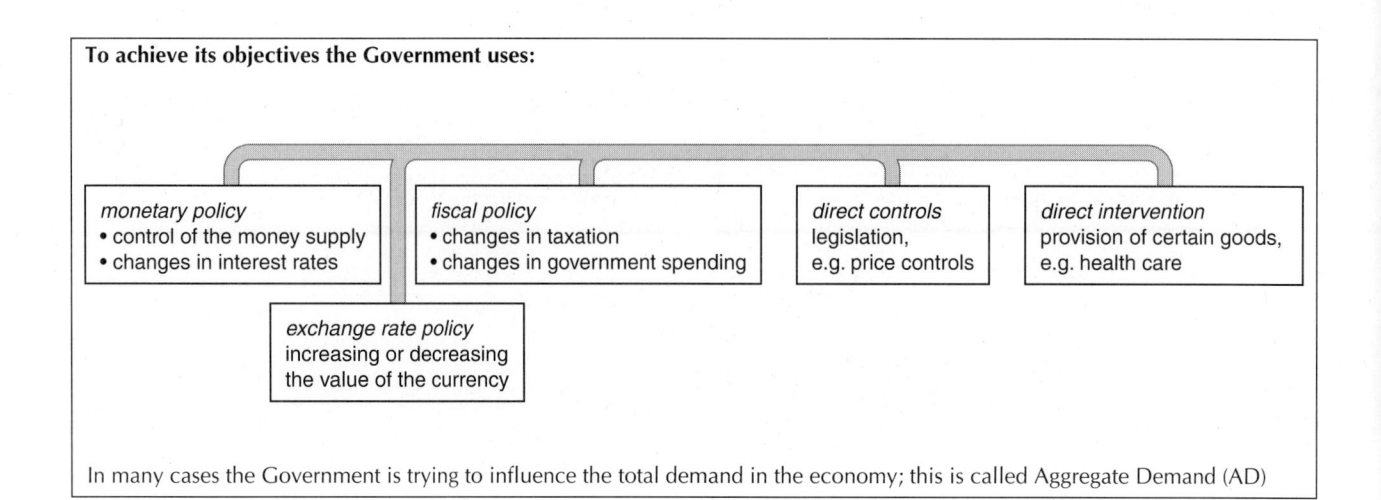

To achieve its objectives the Government uses:

monetary policy
- control of the money supply
- changes in interest rates

fiscal policy
- changes in taxation
- changes in government spending

direct controls
legislation,
e.g. price controls

direct intervention
provision of certain goods,
e.g. health care

exchange rate policy
increasing or decreasing
the value of the currency

In many cases the Government is trying to influence the total demand in the economy; this is called Aggregate Demand (AD)

Taxation

Taxes can be

indirect	placed on the goods or services themselves, e.g. VAT
direct	taken directly from income, e.g. income tax or corporation tax
progressive	take a higher proportion of income as income rises
regressive	take a smaller proportion of income as income rises
specific	certain amount (£) per unit
ad valorem tax	adds a given percentage to the price, e.g. VAT

Tax increases

If indirect taxes increase (e.g. VAT) this makes goods and services more expensive and will usually lead to a fall in sales.

If direct taxes increase (e.g. income tax or corporation tax) firms and/or households have less money to spend. This leads to a fall in demand for goods and services.

Types of economy

```
                    Types of economy
◄─────────────────────────────────────────────────►
```

Free market economy	Mixed economy	Command or planned economy
resources are allocated by market forces of supply and demand	mixture of free market and command economies; has private and public sector	Government allocates resources

The more interventionist a government is, the more it will regulate or interfere with the free market and move towards a command economy. A 'laissez-faire' approach to the economy means that the Government prefers to let the market mechanism work rather than intervene.

Private sector: organisations are controlled by private individuals, e.g. companies

Public sector: organisations are controlled by the Government, e.g. BBC

Problems of free market:
- inequality - can be large differences between rich and poor
- will not provide 'public goods', such as streetlighting; no one would pay for street lighting in a free market - individuals hope someone else will pay for them and that they will benefit anyway. They would try to be 'free riders'. The Government has to provide these goods.
- merit goods are underprovided. These are goods that individuals would not value sufficiently and so would not consume enough of them, e.g. healthcare, education
- instability - prices might fluctuate greatly in some markets, e.g. exchange rates; society might prefer stability
- resources may not reallocate efficiently, e.g if demand changes employees may be left unemployed
- 'external costs'- costs to society which the firm will not pay for in the free market, e.g. pollution; because firms would not account for these external costs they overproduce unless the Government intervenes. The total cost to society is the private costs to the firm + the external cost.

Advantages of free market:
- incentive for producers as they keep the profits
- markets are responsive to consumer demand
- incentive to be efficient to keep costs down
- incentive to be innovative

Problems of command economy:
- lack of incentive as profits belong to the Government
- informational problems
- coordination problems if the Government tries to organise the whole economy.

The trend has been towards free market economies and less Government intervention, e.g privatisation and deregulation in Eastern Europe.

External Factors 59

Types of economy continued

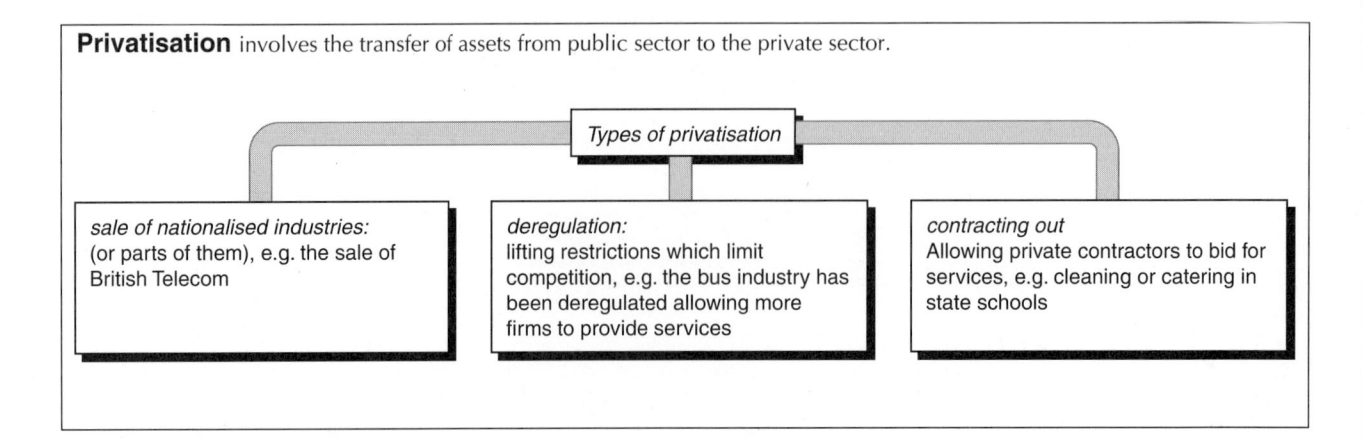

Privatisation involves the transfer of assets from public sector to the private sector.

Types of privatisation

- *sale of nationalised industries:* (or parts of them), e.g. the sale of British Telecom
- *deregulation:* lifting restrictions which limit competition, e.g. the bus industry has been deregulated allowing more firms to provide services
- *contracting out* Allowing private contractors to bid for services, e.g. cleaning or catering in state schools

Reasons against privatisation:
- may create privately owned monopolies e.g. the water companies have monopolies in their regions
- standards and service may suffer as companies aim to increase their profit

Reasons for privatising:
- raises revenue for the Government
- creates more competition
- frees organisations from political influence - decisions were sometimes made for political rather than business reasons
- increases share ownership

Reasons for government ownership of services:
- to prevent private firms exploiting the consumer, e.g. in many countries the water industry is owned by the government to prevent private firms charging high prices
- to provide important services such as health and education; the government wants all people to have access to these services and provides them itself
- to ensure the defence of the country, e.g. defence and nuclear energy
- to protect an industry, e.g. from foreign competition

In the 1980s and early 1990s Government policy:
- privatised many industries
- focused on reducing inflation
- deregulated many businesses
- switched the emphasis from direct to indirect tax
- emphasised the role of the free market

In the 1980s and 1990s the Conservative government privatised many industries, e.g.

		Sold for:
1980-1	British Steel	£509mn
1980-1	British Aerospace	£60mn
1980-1	National Freight Corporation	£100mn
1980-1	British Airways	£160mn
1989-90	Water companies	£5028mn
1994-5	British Coal	£1,633mn

Legal environment

Employment Law includes:

Sex Discrimination Act 1975, 1986: illegal to discriminate against someone because of their sex or marital status. Relates to, e.g. recruitment, terms and conditions, training, promotion, and dismissal.

Race Relations Act, 1976: illegal to discriminate against someone on the basis of race, ethnic group, colour.

Equal Pay Act, 1970: an employee doing the same or broadly similar work as a member of the opposite sex is entitled to equal rates of pay and conditions.

Equal Pay Act (Amendment) 1983: equal pay for work of equal value.

Redundancy Payments Act 1965: Employees who have worked continuously for an organisation for 5 year's part time or 2 years full time are entitled to notice and statutory redundancy pay (approximately 1 week for every year worked)

Health and safety:

Factories Act, 1961: Offices, Shops and Railway Premises Act 1963; these provide minimum requirements for safety.

Health and Safety at Work Act 1974: employers must ensure that as far as is reasonably practicable 'the health, safety and welfare of employees, covers, e.g. plant and working equipment, handling, storage and transportation of articles and substances, training and supervision

Enforced by Health and Safety Executive: can enter premises; can order improvements to be made.

Data Protection Act, 1984

to 'regulate the use of automatically processed information relating to an individual'

All users of personal data must register with the Registrar. Law states e.g. data should be adequate, relevant and not excessive; individuals are entitled to reasonable access; data should be accurate and up to date.

Competition Policy:

Responsibility of Office of Fair Trading which attempts to control anti competitive behaviour and protect consumers.

Legislation includes: 1948 Competition Act; 1973 Fair Trading Act.

Monopolies and Mergers Commission: recommends whether a monopoly or proposed merger is in the public interest. A monopoly exists if a firm has more than 25% of the market. Monopolies are referred to the MMC by the Office of Fair Trading; MMC can recommend that a merger is prohibited or, that firms end certain types of uncompetitive behaviour.

Restrictive trade practices: include price fixing and market sharing agreements. All restrictive practices have to be registered with the Office of Fair Trading. The Restrictive Practices Court decides whether to allow an agreement. It may be allowed if, e.g. it prevents local unemployment; operates against existing restrictions or maintains exports.

Consumer Law: includes

Weights and Measures Act, 1951: inspectors can test weighing and measuring equipment of organisations e.g. scales and petrol pumps.

Trade Descriptions Act, 1968: prohibits false or misleading descriptions of goods or services. It is a criminal offence to lie about a good's weight, size and contents.

Sale of Goods Act, 1979: goods must be 'of merchantable quality' (i.e. no serious flaws), 'fit for the purpose' (i.e. can do what it is supposed to), and 'as described'.

Supply of Goods and Services Act, 1982: this extends the 1979 Sale of Goods Act to cover services. These must be 'merchantable quality' and at 'reasonable rates'.

Consumer Protection Act, 1987: firms are liable for any damage which their defective goods might cause unless they can prove the danger could not be foreseen.

Consumer Credit Act 1974: anyone offering credit must seek a licence from the Director General of Fair Trading and state the annual percentage rate of interest charged (APR)

Unsolicited Goods and Services Act, 1971: prevents firms delivering unordered items and then asking for payment.

Food and Drugs Act: protects the consumer by making the sale of unfit food a criminal offence; also contains labelling and hygiene regulations

Unfair Contract Terms Act, 1977: the seller cannot use exclusion clauses to remove customers' legal rights

Fair Trading Act, 1973: This established the Office of Fair Trading (OFT) to protect customers against unfair practices.

The OFT:
- publishes information so consumers know their rights
- prosecutes traders who break the law
- recommends to the Monopolies and Mergers Commission that certain firms or markets should be investigated.

Most consumer legislation is enforced by local councils through departments such as the Trading Standards Department and Environmental Health Department.

Contract Law: a contract is a legally binding agreement between two or more persons. If a contract is breached, the aggrieved party can seek damages or sue for 'specific performance'.

Tort: a tort is a 'civil wrong'; this includes a variety of activities such as negligence, e.g. if an employee is negligent; the employer can be liable as well (called vicarious liability).

Economic environment

National Income
income in an economy is usually measured by

GDP: Gross Domestic Product-value of final goods and services produced in an economy. This shows how much has been earned within a country.

In a recession (when National Income falls):
- demand for a firm's products may fall
- firms may have to cut back on overtime or make redundancies
- consumers may be more price sensitive
- stocks may increase and firms may have to decrease production

The effect of a recession depends on the size of the recession, the length of the recession, and the type of firm, e.g. food and pharmaceutical industries are fairly recession proof, whereas the housing, construction and car industries are sensitive to income changes. Luxury goods will be more sensitive than necessities to changes in the level of national income.

Trade Cycle (Business cycle)

Over time the economy usually goes through booms and slumps. This is called the 'trade cycle' or 'business cycle'.

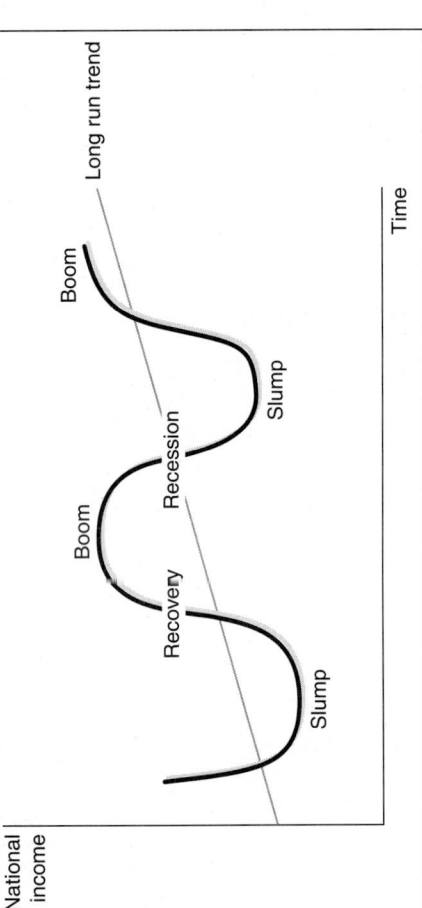

Interest rates
the cost of borrowing money and the reward offered to savers.

If interest rates increase:
- households are more likely to save and less likely to spend.
- households discretionary income is likely to fall as more money is used to repay mortgages and loans (discretionary income = income after tax and regular bills)
- firms are likely to reduce their stocks because money tied up in stocks represents a greater opportunity cost
- debtors will want to hold onto their money to earn interest and are likely to delay payment
- creditors will want their money more quickly
- because of an increased desire to save in the UK the exchange rate might increase

If interest rates decrease:
With lower interest rates households and firms are more likely to borrow. Spending and demand for most goods and services should increase; firms may increase investment because borrowing is cheaper.

Exchange rates
The exchange rate is the price of one currency in terms of another, e.g. it may cost 3 Deutschmarks to buy one pound.

If demand increases the price is likely to increase. If supply increases the price is likely to fall as more are available.

An increase in the price of a pound in foreign currency is called an APPRECIATION; it means the pound is stronger.

$£1 = 3DM$ Strong pound

A fall in the price of a pound in foreign currency is called a DEPRECIATION; it means the pound is weaker.

$£1 = 2DM$ Weak pound

A strong pound is expensive in terms of foreign currency

The effect of an increase in the pound:
- increases price of UK goods and services abroad; in terms of foreign currency; demand is likely to fall. The extent of the fall depends on how sensitive demand is to price (price elasticity of demand). However, some firms may decide not to increase price and accept lower profits
- imports become cheaper in pounds; may reduce input costs; may make it more difficult for domestic firms to compete against foreign competitors
- depends on how much pound has gone up and for how long
- depends which currencies it has increased against

62 External Factors

Unemployment

Unemployment:
Measured by the number of people claiming unemployment benefit.

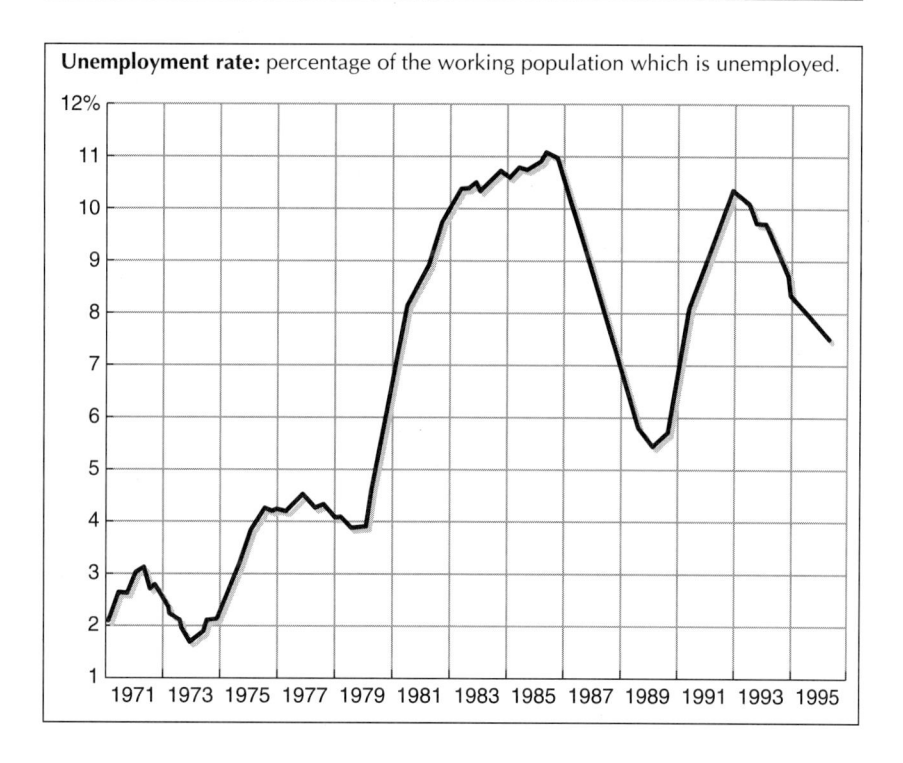

Unemployment rate: percentage of the working population which is unemployed.

Types of unemployment include:

- structural - people are unemployed because of the changing structure of the economy, e.g. a miner may not have the correct skills for the new jobs being created in computing.
- seasonal - people in jobs such as fruit picking are likely to be unemployed at certain times of the year.
- frictional - people between jobs, i.e. left one job and waiting before accepting another.
- residual - people who are unwilling to work or unable because of a disability
- cyclical - people are unemployed because of a lack of demand. Also called 'demand deficient' or Keynesian.

High unemployment may mean:

- less demand for goods and services
- a wider choice of labour for a firm
- a more co-operative workforce as employees are worried about their jobs

The effect of an increase in unemployment on a firm depends on:

- to what extent has unemployment increased?
- how long will the increase last for?
- in what areas has the unemployment occurred?
- what types of people are unemployed, e.g. what skills?
- is the firm aiming to expand?

Deindustrialisation

This refers to the decline of manufacturing in the UK. This has led to high levels of structural unemployment because employees are made redundant and do not have the skills which are now needed by British firms. The main growth sectors in the UK are in the service sector and so employees need to retrain to get jobs.

Much of the decline in manufacturing has occurred in particular regions and has caused high levels of regional unemployment. To reduce unemployment the government must improve the mobility of labour.

Geographical mobility

People are sometimes reluctant to move areas because of:

- removal costs
- family ties
- the high cost of housing in the areas with more jobs

Occupational mobility

People cannot always accept jobs because they do not have the right skills. Occupational mobility means that people can move from one job to another. This requires training.

External Factors 63

International Trade

Based on comparative advantage; countries specialise in producing goods or services in which they have a comparative advantage, i.e. a lower opportunity cost

Free trade: no barriers to trade. The benefits should be wider choice for consumers and lower costs.

Free trade area: members remove barriers to trade amongst themselves, e.g. LAFTA - the Latin American Free Trade Area. Members can set their own tariffs with non members.

Customs Union: free trade amongst members and a common external tariff with non member countries, e.g. European Union.

Barriers to trade (protectionism):

- quotas - limit on quantity of goods allowed into a country
- tariffs - tax placed on imports
- technical barriers - regulations which make it difficult for foreign producers to sell their products
- exchange controls - limits on the amount of currency that can be changed into foreign currency to buy foreign goods.
- embargo - a ban on all trade in a particular good or service
- subsidies (i.e. giving grants) - by subsidising a UK firm, the Government helps it to compete with foreign companies

Trade war: countries use protectionist measures against each other.

World Trade Organisation: member countries aim to reduce barriers to trade.

International competitiveness:

Depends on factors such as:

- price relative to competitors - the exchange rate can have a major influence on this
- quality of product (i.e. to what extent does it meet customer needs?)
- reliability of the product
- overall service, e.g. delivery times

Why protect UK companies?

- save jobs in particular industries
- give small firms time to grow and improve (infant industries)
- to maintain a way of life (e.g. farming)
- to keep control of strategically important industries, e.g. defence industries
- retaliation
- to raise revenue (from tariffs)
- to prevent foreign firms 'dumping' (selling their goods at a very low price to gain control of a market)

Balance of payments: revenue generated from exports sold abroad – spending on imports. Balance of payments surplus = more is spent on a country's exports than it spends on imports. Balance of payments deficit = country spends more on imports than it receives from exports.

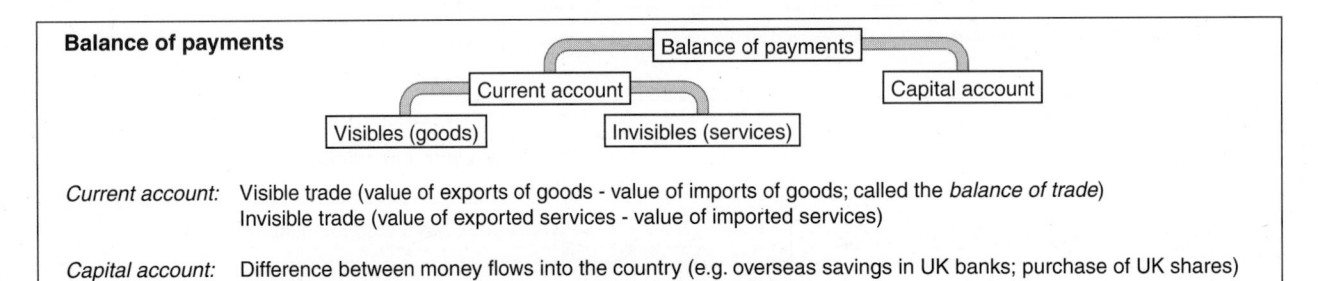

Balance of payments

Balance of payments → Current account (Visibles (goods), Invisibles (services)) + Capital account

Current account: Visible trade (value of exports of goods - value of imports of goods; called the *balance of trade*)
Invisible trade (value of exported services - value of imported services)

Capital account: Difference between money flows into the country (e.g. overseas savings in UK banks; purchase of UK shares) and money flows out of the country (e.g. UK savings overseas)

Exports: goods and services sold abroad

Imports: goods and services bought from abroad

Advantages of trade

- more goods and services available for consumers
- firms have bigger markets where they can sell their products
- greater pressure on firms to be efficient (so they can compete internationally)

64 External Factors

International Trade continued

Export documents

- bill of lading - contains details of the goods being shipped including the destination and the ship they are travelling on.
- export invoice - this is the bill which is sent to the customer
- certificate of origin - proves where the goods have come from
- certificate of value - proves that the goods are worth the amount stated on the bill of lading
- HM Customs declaration - signed statement of what the containers contain
- certificate of insurance - this is needed by the company transporting the goods so they know the goods are insured in case anything happens
- export licence - this is needed for certain types of goods, e.g. permission might be needed to export weapons.

Payment for exports

Trading overseas can be risky. In particular, UK firms are often worried about receiving payment for their goods. Chasing bad debts abroad can be expensive and time consuming.

Methods of ensuring payment include:

- payment with order - under this system buyers must pay in advance. Unfortunately very few buyers will be willing to do this.
- draft (also called a bill of exchange) - with a 'sight draft' the seller produces a document which states that the buyer will pay as soon as the goods are delivered. With a 'term draft' the buyer will be given a certain number of days (e.g. 30 or 60) to pay.
- letter of credit - these are arranged by the buyer's bank and the seller's bank and cannot usually be cancelled once signed, so the seller is certain to receive the money.

Export Credits Guarantee Department (ECGD)

This is an organisation set up by the Government to help exporters. The ECGD offers an insurance scheme; in return for a premium the Government pays most of any bad debts which occur depending on the particular country and customer.

British Overseas Trade Board (BOTB)

A Government organisation which provides:

- information and advice on foreign markets
- introductions to contacts
- market research on overseas markets
- help promoting products and services abroad through its Trade Fairs Overseas Scheme
- use of its Statistics and Market Intelligence Library

UNCTAD

(United Nations Conference on Trade and Development) aims to encourage richer, developed nations to help poorer countries, e.g.
- by stabilising prices of commodities such as copper
- provide aid to underdeveloped countries
- reduce barriers to trade from these countries (e.g. exports)

IMF

International Monetary Fund

Aims to
- stabilise exchange rates
- help countries with balance of payments problems
- encourage world trade

Problems exporting

- lack of information about the market and its customers
- language problems, e.g. completing the necessary forms, producing adverts
- risk of not being paid; if customers do not pay it can be difficult getting the money
- different laws in different countries
- fluctuations in the exchange rate; changes in the exchange rate can alter the price of UK goods in foreign currencies and make imports more expensive to buy.
- additional costs, e.g. for transportation, to adjust the product to meet other countries' standards

Europe

The European Economic Community was set up to create a free trade area in which member states would trade without quotas and tariffs. By 1986 it was obvious that some barriers still existed, e.g. differences in regulations made it difficult to transport goods from one country to another. The aim of the Single European Act was to create an area in which there was freedom of movement of goods, services, labours and capital. Member countries were given until 1992 to bring this about. The result was a harmonisation of regulations.

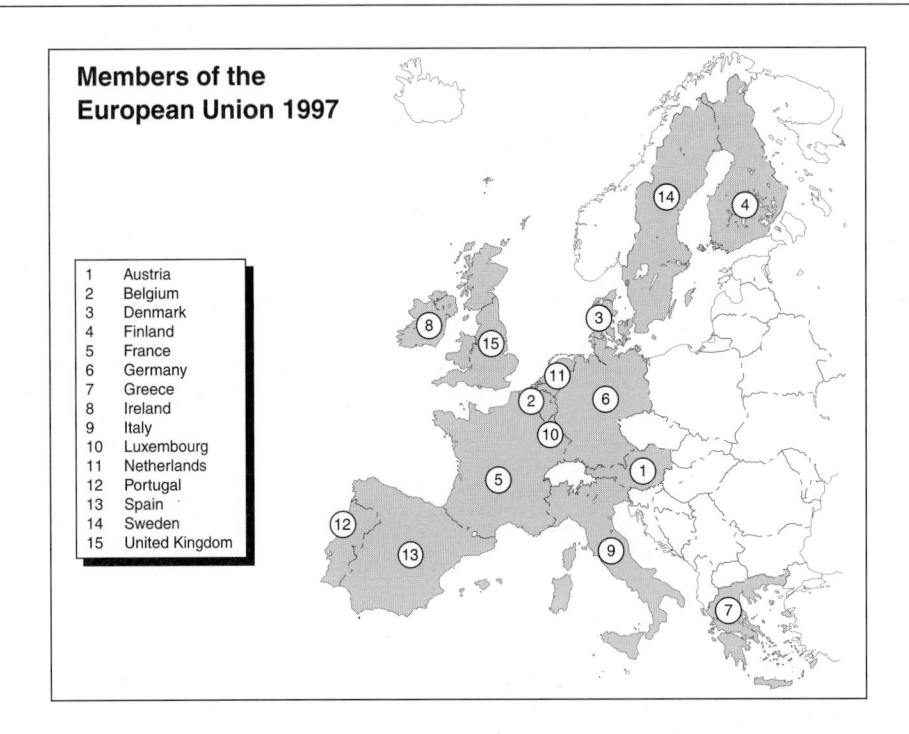

Members of the European Union 1997

1	Austria
2	Belgium
3	Denmark
4	Finland
5	France
6	Germany
7	Greece
8	Ireland
9	Italy
10	Luxembourg
11	Netherlands
12	Portugal
13	Spain
14	Sweden
15	United Kingdom

Membership

In 1997 there were 15 members of the European Union: Belgium, France, Germany, Italy, Luxembourg, the Netherlands, Denmark, Iceland, the UK, Greece, Portugal, Spain, Austria, Finland and Sweden. A number of other countries in central and eastern Europe have applied for membership and are likely to join in the near future (e.g. Turkey, Poland, Hungary, Romania).

Key dates:
- 1957 European Economic Community set up.
- 1973 UK joined European Union
- 1986 Single European Act; aimed to create 'an area without internal frontiers in which the free movement of goods, persons, services and capital is ensured.'
- 1990 UK joins Exchange Rate Mechanism; the value of each currency is fixed against other member currencies
- 1992 Maastricht Treaty, member states agreed to go ahead with a single currency
- 1992 UK leaves Exchange Rate Mechanism

European Union institutions:

The Council of Ministers: the European Union's decision making body. It agrees legislation based on proposals from the Commission. There are, in fact, several councils (e.g foreign affairs, agriculture, finance); attended by the relevant ministers from member states and by the Commission.

The Commission:
- proposes community policy and legislation
- implements decisions taken by the Council of Ministers

Consists of commissioners appointed by the member governments.

The European Parliament: directly elected every five years. Consulted on proposals for EC law. Can influence shape of laws and has power of veto in certain areas.

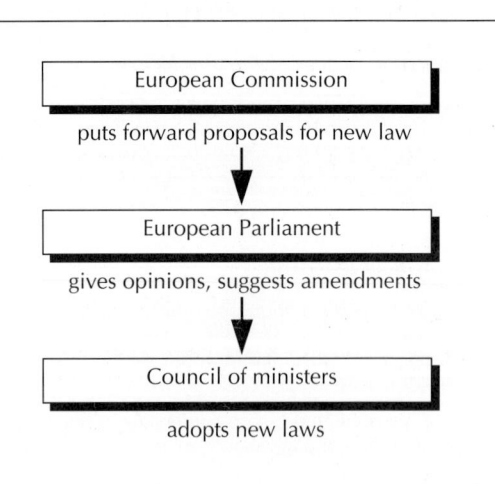

European Commission
↓ puts forward proposals for new law
European Parliament
↓ gives opinions, suggests amendments
Council of ministers
adopts new laws

Europe continued

The European Union provides UK firms with:

- bigger markets; potential for growth and economies of scale
- more market opportunities
- more sources of employees
- greater competition
- more sources of finance
- incentive and opportunity to become efficient and learn from other firms
- the same safety and technical standards for many products
- the ability to compete for contracts from member governments
- the removal of border controls and lower administration costs.

Social Chapter (part of Maastricht treaty): proposals for employees concerning conditions, participation, working hours, protection of children, disabled persons, collective bargaining.

Common Agricultural Policy: scheme to maintain the price of foodstuffs in Europe. If too much is produced the European Union buys up the excess to prevent the price falling below a set level. In practice the intervention price has been set too high in the past so that the Union has had to buy up food to stop the price falling. This has led to large stocks building up, e.g. wine lakes and butter mountains. Imports of agricultural products from outside of the EU have a tax (tariff) placed on them.

European Monetary Union

All members of the European Union (except the UK) have agreed to monetary union. This should lead to a single currency in Europe. This currency is called the 'Euro'

Benefits of a single currency

- saves money because people do not have to pay commission to change their currency into other currencies
- stability for businesses: if exchange rates are allowed to fluctuate firms do not know exactly how much goods from abroad will cost them or what their goods will sell for in foreign currencies

The EU and business

The EU affects businesses in many areas. For example,

- agriculture - the EU spends large sums of money on its Common Agriculture Policy. This affects what farmers grow, the prices they receive and the grants they get.
- unemployment - regions which suffer from high unemployment can receive grants from the EU
- Social Fund - this fund is used to finance retraining.
- transport - money is spent to support the development of a country's infrastructure, e.g. motorways, railways and canals.

The European Union also helps via:

- The European Investment Bank - this provides finance for small and medium sized businesses.
- Competition Policy - this protects the consumer.
- Social Rights; member countries have agreed to certain rights for employees e.g. the right to join a trade union, the right to equal treatment for men and women, the right to health and safety protection
- Consumer rights e.g. safety, quality and hygiene standards. There are also regulations on labelling and packaging.
- regulations on waste, noise levels, pollution levels

Social environment

The social environment: includes the values, attitudes, needs and expectations of consumers, employees, the Government, pressure groups, and investors. The social environment also includes demographic factors, such as the size of the population and its age structure.

Recent social trends in the UK include:

- growing environmentalism
- growing interest in health and fitness
- growing concern about the ethics of organisations
- more leisure time
- earlier retirement
- more women in the workforce
- more job mobility - people change jobs more often
- more need for training
- better living standards
- slow population growth in UK
- decline in availability of younger workers
- ageing population
- more skilled and educated workforce
- more temporary and part time employment

The effect of changing social trends depends on:

- the type of firm, e.g. Mothercare will be affected by birth rates; retirement homes will be affected by the ageing population
- the size of trend and how long it lasts, e.g. will consumers still be concerned about ethics if the economy goes into a recession?

Statistics

The UK population is increasing at a slow rate:

Year	Population (000s)
1984	56506
1985	56685
1986	56852
1987	57009
1988	57158
1989	57358
1990	57561
1991	57808
1992	58006
1993	58191
1994	58395

Source CSO Office of Population Censuses and Surveys

Age structure of the UK (1991):

	%
under 16	20.3
16–39	35.2
40–64	28.7
65–79	12.0
80+	3.7
Total	100

Source: Social Trends

- Ethnic minorities form around 5% of the UKs population
- Over 25% of all households in the UK are people living alone

People are increasingly concerned about their health

People now have more leisure time

68 External Factors

Pressure groups

Pressure groups:
Organisations formed by people with a shared interest, which seek to influence public opinion and Government policy.

Interest groups: established to serve the interests of members, e.g. trade unions

Cause groups: established to promote a cause, e.g. environmentalist groups such as Greenpeace, Friends of the Earth

Other examples of pressure groups:

Institute of Directors: employers' pressure group; lobbies Government

Institute of Management: professional association of managers

Employer's Associations: employers' organisations for employers in the same industry.

The Consumers' Association: represents the interests of consumers; tests products to find the best value for money; tests safety of products; provides advice for consumers on their rights; publishes the results in 'Which?' magazine.

Trade Unions: represent employees' interests; seek to represent and protect employees in discussions and negotiations with management.

Environmental groups: put pressure on firms to consider the environmental impact of their production. Examples of such groups are Greenpeace and Friends of the Earth.

Automobile Association (AA) and Royal Automobile Club (RAC): motoring organisations which campaign on behalf of the motorist.

The Media: e.g. television and newspapers. Report on business issues and what firms are doing. Try to expose scandals or stories which will interest their viewers or readers.

Pressure group activities include:

- boycotting products, e.g. do not buy animal fur products
- media campaign, e.g. 1996 Greenpeace pressurised Shell into not dumping the Brent Spar oil rig in the sea
- lobbying government, i.e. putting views across, e.g. the brewers lobbied Government to change its legislation on ownership of pubs in the 1980s
- demonstrations and petitions

Environmental issues include:

- waste minimisation
- recycling
- energy efficiency
- protecting the ozone layer
- environmental labelling

BS7750: certificate which is awarded to firms achieving acceptable environmental standards.

Social audit: assessment of the effect of the firm's activities on society, e.g. amount of pollution, waste

---

Insider pressure groups: are regularly consulted by the Government, e.g. British Medical Association.

Outsider groups: do not have such easy access to the Government.

Effectiveness of pressure groups depends on:

- number of members
- resources
- public support
- ability to influence media and politicians

Ethics: a view about what is right and wrong, what is moral

Ethical issues include:

- should firms use child labour?
- what wages should firms pay in the Third World?
- to what extent should firms seek to be environmentally friendly?
- should firms get involved in certain activities, e.g. making weapons?

Why should organisations behave ethically?

- because their owners want them to
- to attract ethical investors, e.g. the CoOp Bank
- to attract ethical consumers
- to attract employees
- to avoid unfavourable media attention

Why should firms not behave ethically?

- they do not have to provided they behave legally
- it can impose extra costs
- there is no agreement on what is ethical
- can be conflict of interests, e.g. by not producing cigarettes they may have to make employees redundant

External Factors

Change

Change is the one constant: there are always new markets, new products, new processes, new values and attitudes and developments in technology. Some firms embrace change - others resist it.

Internal change includes: employees' motives, behaviour, skills, product design

External change includes: PEST factors - political, economic, social, and technological

Resistance to change occurs because individuals:
- may not see the point
- prefer the existing arrangements, change may involve extra effort
- are afraid that they will not be able to perform as well in new situation; uncertain of their abilities
- do not think that the proposed change is appropriate

Reaction to change can include: fear, resentment, frustration, and anger.

Some people resist change

Fear   Anger   Frustration

Managing change:

Change is easier if you tell people why it is happening, listen to their views and make sure they can cope

- plan carefully
- show benefits of it
- pay attention to speed of change
- negotiate
- explain need and purpose of it
- involve employees in it
- train
- if necessary, coerce and force change through

Change creates opportunities

for example:
- new skills
- new jobs
- new products
- new ways of doing things

Changes in UK industry
- deindustrialisation - over the last hundred years there has been a decline in the importance of the UK's manufacturing sector; this is known as deindustrialisation
- more technology - for example, many businesses now use information technology
- more trade - many markets have opened up to trade this century; for example, it is much easier to trade within the European Union and with eastern Europe
- developing products has become much faster, e.g. firms use Computer Aided Design to speed up the design process of new products; many products we use every day are relatively new, e.g. mobile 'phone, satellite television, fax machines, personal computers

Communication

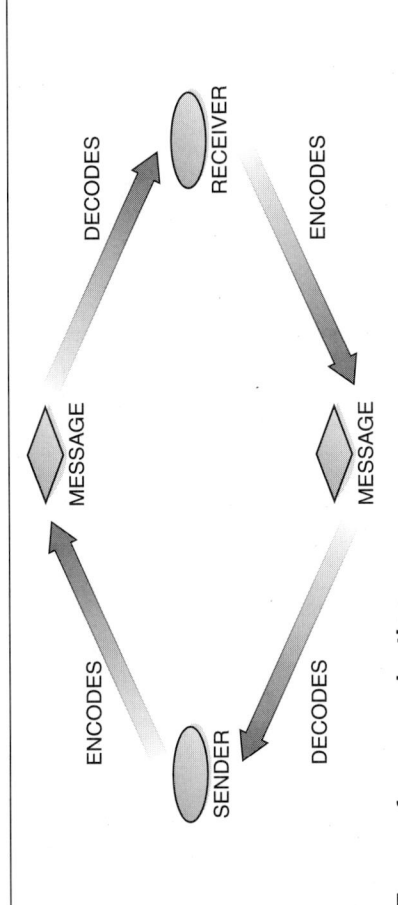

```
SENDER → ENCODES → MESSAGE → (to) RECEIVER → DECODES
RECEIVER → ENCODES → MESSAGE → (to) SENDER → DECODES
```

Types of communication

Vertical: up and down the organisation; downward is from superiors to subordinates e.g. giving orders, setting targets; upward is employee to employer, e.g. presenting a report

Lateral: communication across the organisation, e.g. one team member to another

Verbal: using words (whether they are spoken or written down)

Non verbal: not using words, e.g. body language

Formal: using the channels of communication established by the organisation.

Informal: using channels established by the employees themselves. Often called the grapevine. Passes information around quickly but information is often distorted

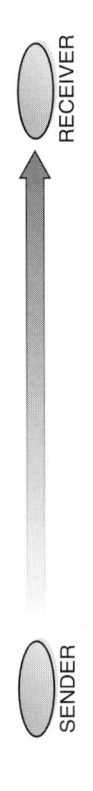

One way: sender does not receive feedback, e.g. manager puts up notice on noticeboard

SENDER → RECEIVER

Two way: sender receives feedback, e.g. manager discusses an issue with an employee at a meeting,
Slower than one way but sender gains more information

SENDER ⇄ RECEIVER

Managers must communicate with

- employees
- shareholders
- banks
- suppliers
- local community
- media
- potential investors
- government

Barriers to communication:

Jargon - words or phrases not known to the receiver

Noise - any form of interference which makes it difficult to receive, e.g. actual noise or use of complicated words

Emotional state - if the receiver is upset, angry or depressed he or she can misinterpret

Distrust - if employees do not trust their employer, this affects their interpretation of the message

Suitability of the channel - e.g. a long list of sales figures might be easier to understand if written down.

Location - e.g. communication is more difficult if parts of the business are on different sites.

Results of poor communication:

- low morale
- high level of errors
- hostile relations
- lack of control

Communication is important

- with employees so that they know what they are expected to do and why; they also need to know how they are getting on
- with shareholders so that they know how the firm is performing
- with suppliers so they know what the firm wants, when they will be paid and if the firm is satisfied with its supplies
- with customers so that they know what the firm has to offer and why it is worth buying

Information and Communication 71

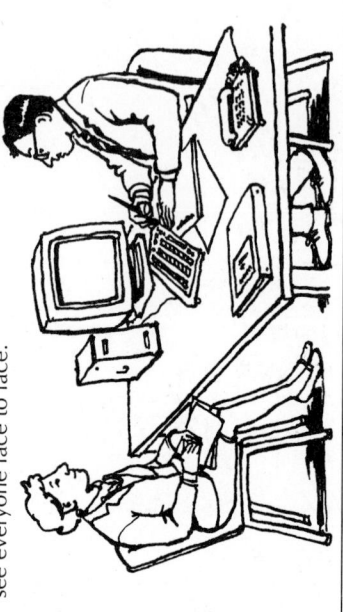

Communication continued

Internal communication

This occurs within the firm. For example:

- management explain their plans to employees
- employees bargain with managers over pay and working conditions
- different departments communicate with each other

Good internal communication makes sure everyone within the firm is aiming towards the same goal. It makes sure people know what they are expected to do and why they are doing it. It also co-ordinates the activities of different parts of the business.

External communication

This occurs when a firm communicates with individuals and groups outside of the firm. For example:

- the Government needs information on a company's profits
- customers need information about the company's products or services
- potential investors need to know how the company is doing
- existing investors need to know how the company is being run and what it has achieved

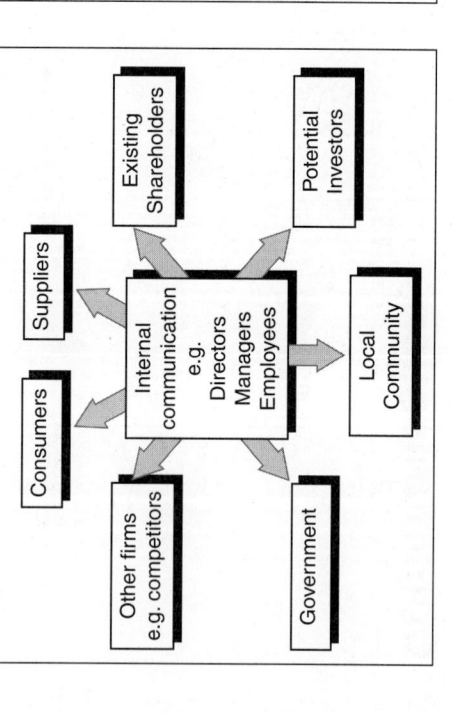

```
                    Existing
                    Shareholders
 Other firms                          Suppliers
 e.g. competitors
              Internal
              communication
              e.g.
              Directors
              Managers
              Employees
 Government                           Consumers
                    Local
                    Community
                    Potential
                    Investors
```

Written communication

letters and memos:

letters – usually formal and not used within the firm

Jo-Jo Design
37 High Street
Oxford OX3 7FL

5/6/97

Dear Mr Taylor,

I am writing to confirm our meeting at 1.30 pm on Monday 10th June at our offices here in Oxford.

I look forward to seeing you then.

Yours sincerely,

A. Boulon

A. Boulon

---

memos – an informal type of letter usually used within the firm. Generally fairly informal in terms of the way they are expressed but may still be important.

MEMO

From: Bob Smith   To: Tom Graham

C.C.   Fabienne Cholsey   Date   25/2/97

I've now fixed up a meeting with James Taylor from Entro Ltd. I'm seeing him next Monday and will report back after then.

---

reports: detailed written communications on a specific subject. Usually contain the following sections:

- objectives of the report
- conclusion
- findings
- recommendations

agenda for meeting: this sets out what issues are to be discussed at a meeting. The agenda usually has:

- apologies for absences
- matters arising – this allows anyone present to raise any issues from earlier meetings
- main points for discussion
- any other business: any issue anyone wants to discuss which is not on the agenda
- date of next meeting

minutes: are written after a meeting and are a record of what happened and what was agreed.

Oral communication

telephone: faster means of communicating than a letter or memo and more flexible; however not as effective if the message involves large quantities of data or of you need a written record (e.g. a contract of employment). With mobile telephones people can be contacted almost anywhere by telephone nowadays.

face to face: e.g. in interviews and meetings. This is probably the most effective means of communication because you can see how someone is reacting to what you say. Good face to face communication is vital in jobs such as selling. Unfortunately in large firms it is not possible to see everyone face to face.

annual report: every company must publish an annual report and set of accounts and send these to all the shareholders. They contain details of the company's financial performance and information from the directors about how the company has done and its plans for the future.

newsletters: these are sent out to the customers to provide information on the company and any new developments such as new products. Newsletters can also be used internally to keep employees informed about changes in the firm.

noticeboards: used to provide information for staff; the problem is that notices are often left on the board for a long time and it is difficult to see what is relevant and what is not.

72 Information and Communication

Communication continued

Visual communication

Firms pay a great deal of attention to the design of their product, their logo, their stationery and even the painting of their vans. All of these send out signals to the consumer.

Visual communication also involves the way that data is presented, e.g. if you are trying to highlight a trend in sales it is often better to use a chart rather than a list of numbers. Types of charts include: Bar charts, pie charts and line graphs.

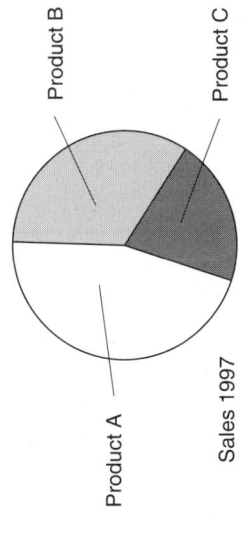

Pie chart showing breakdown of sales

Line graph showing total sales over time

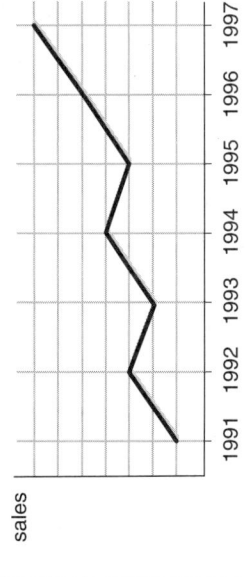

Bar chart showing sales of different regions

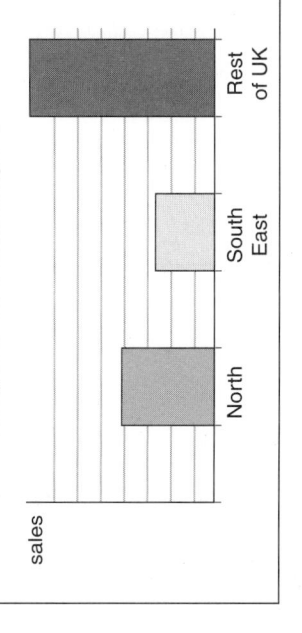

Electronic communication

computers: computers can be linked by being on a network; by using a modem, computers in different locations can be linked via the telephone lines. Firms can get data using a computer by accessing a database, e.g. firms can access the INTERNET if they have a computer, the appropriate software and a modem.

fax: this transmits pages to another fax machine using the telephone system. It is a fast means of communication.

electronic mail (e mail): relatively cheap and very quick method of communicating from one computer terminal to another. The message is typed on screen and transmitted to someone else's electronic mailbox; if their machine is turned off a sign showing that an e mail is waiting will show when they turn it on next time.

video conferencing: a camera films one person or a group of people at one location and transmits this image to people in another place (and vice versa). Via the cameras the two groups can hold a meeting.

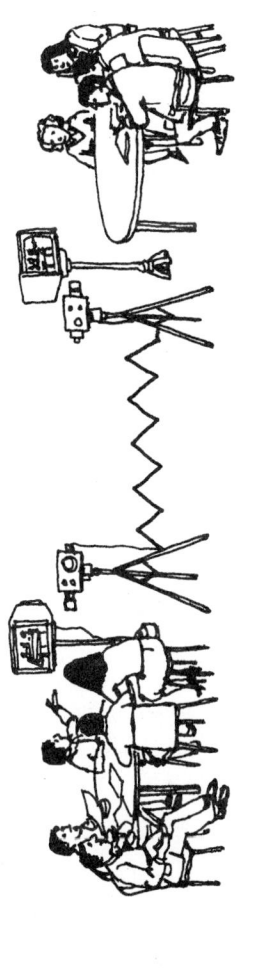

Information and Communication 73

Information technology

> **Information technology:** the collection, storage, processing, and communication of information by electronic means.
>
> Enables large quantities of information to be handled quickly and economically.

Benefits of information technology:
- quicker handling of data
- better decision making because of easier access to information
- ability to consider 'what if'? scenarios easily
- increased productivity
- less waste

Information as a resource:
- essential for planning, organising, motivating, and controlling
- can provide a competitive advantage
- can improve performance and productivity

What is 'good' information?
- reliable
- accurate
- intelligible
- up to date
- complete
- appropriate level of detail
- available in a useful format
- cost effective

Problems with information technology:
- cost of selection, installation, maintenance
- training and retraining

Uses of information technology:

Data management: enables more effective maintenance, updating, and manipulation of data, e.g. keeping of personnel and financial records

Communication: enables easier communication between people, e.g. fax machines, mobile phones

Manufacturing: used in systems such as computer integrated manufacture, can improve areas such as quality control, materials handling and stock control

Decision support: enables better decisions by collecting, analysing and manipulating data more effectively

Office automation: more effective performance with increased use of spreadsheets, word processors, desktop publishers, and telecommunications links such as electronic mail.

Word processor: performs similar functions to a typewriter but it is easier to change words, sentences or paragraphs. Most have additional features such as spellcheckers. By using a database and a word processing package together, the firm can undertake mailmergers which produce personalised letters to large numbers of people

Database: set of files organised to enable easy access, e.g. personnel or customer records. Used to keep information such as lists of customers. This information can easily be sorted in different ways e.g. alphabetically or by region

Spreadsheets: used for calculations and manipulating figures e.g. calculating profits. Allow managers to set up mathematical models and investigate effects of different strategies, i.e. analyse 'what if'? questions

Accounts packages: used to computerise the firm's accounts

Communications packages: used to link computers together, e.g. to use the internet

Fax: technique for transmitting text and black and white pictures over the telephone network

Electronic mail: way of sending text messages via a computer network

EDI: electronic data interchange between organisations

EPOS: electronic point of sale e.g. scanning equipment at supermarket check-outs

CD ROM: compact discs for read only data storage i.e. data can be taken off a CD ROM but not added to it

Bar code: a code in the form of parallel lines of varying widths which is used to enter data into computer via a scanner

Video conferencing: method of holding conferences via telecommunications network; individuals can see and hear each other

Software: set of instructions which the computer follows so that it can work

Operating system: vital piece of software which tells the computer how to deal with other programs

Customised software: software which is adapted or designed to suit a particular firm's requirements

---

Management information systems:
provide information for planning and control, e.g. sales figures

Expert systems: cover a particular area of expertise and draw conclusions from computer stored knowledge obtained from specialists. Their purpose is to capture the expertise of key people and make their knowledge available to users of the programme, e.g. used by doctors to diagnose patients' symptoms

Information technology continued

Networks

Systems linking desktop terminals to each other. These are often called local area networks (LANs). Messages for one or several LAN terminals are moved around the network by a central processor.

Networks enable messages to be sent almost instantaneously from one terminal to another. This speeds up communication between employees who are on the network.

A local area network (LAN) consists of:
- a high speed cable connecting the terminals
- a network card (or circuit board) for each terminal which is connected to the network
- network software which manages the transmission of data around the network cabling

A local area network can be used to :
- download data held in the firm's database
- share resources/information on the network
- use electronic mail to send messages to other terminals

LANs can only transmit data within the organisation. To transmit data outside of the organisation a wide area network (WAN) must be used.

Control systems

Use a computer to monitor readings from sensors and send appropriate control signals, e.g. in a greenhouse a control system might monitor the temperature and adjust the ventilation and heating as required.

Control systems:
- involve lower labour costs
- are more reliable than people
- can be put in situations which would be dangerous for people

Data processing

These systems deal with high volume routine tasks, e.g. processing data on sales, purchases or stocks. For example, sales transactions may be entered onto the computer; this can lead to invoices and delivery notes being produced automatically as well as a production plan. A management report summarising the sales transactions will be produced at regular intervals.

On line

Directly linked to a central processing unit (computer). Operations are carried out by instructions which are generated as the computer is being used, e.g. airline booking systems; larger travel agents have their own terminals linked to the airlines' computers which can show spaces available and make reservations.

Off line

Not under the control of a computer's central processing unit e.g. if a terminal is disconnected from the computer it is off line.

Real time

The computer processes the data at the same time as the data is being generated. For example, you can see the prices of shares changing on the computer screen as they actually change at the Stock Exchange.

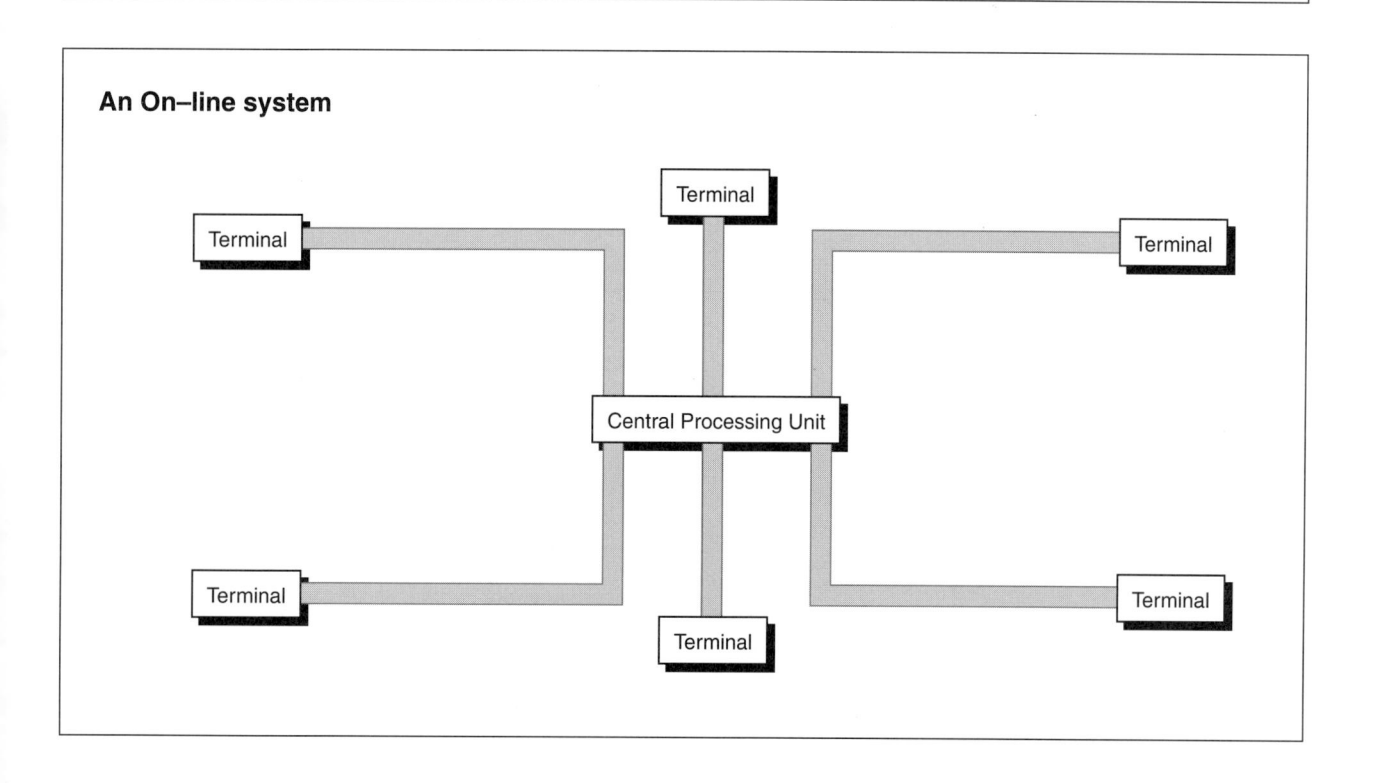

An On–line system

[Diagram: Six Terminals connected to a Central Processing Unit]

Information and Communication 75

Business documents

> Business documents act as a record of transactions and as proof that the transaction took place.

Business documents

- **letterheads** – these are printed with the firm's name, address, telephone, e mail and fax plus any other information which is needed for a limited company such as the registered number, registered office and the directors' names.
- **compliment slips** – usually sent out with brochures or leaflets. Small slips of paper with the company's name and the words 'with thanks' printed on them.
- **business cards** – cards with company's name and address and name and position of the person on them. Given out to clients and contacts.
- **enquiry letter** – letter asking for information from the supplier, e.g. asking for details of price, delivery and specification of the products
- **quotation** – the seller sends a quotation to the enquirer giving details of the terms of sale, e.g. the price and likely delivery time

```
Order form                    Order No    3216
Henley Ltd                    Date:       02/05/97
251 Warehouse St              Reference:  3835L
Oxford

Please Supply
PDM Ltd.
3 Looker Rd
Eynsham

With the following goods
```

Quantity	Description of goods (including stock number)	Unit Price £	Total Value £
2	Telephone Answering Machines 3LM	55	110

- **order form** – this is used to order goods from the seller
- **advice note** – this provides details of the goods which are going to be sent for the customer to check
- **consignment note** – this is used if a firm does not deliver its own goods. A consignment note is sent to the transportation firm with details of where the goods are to be delivered.

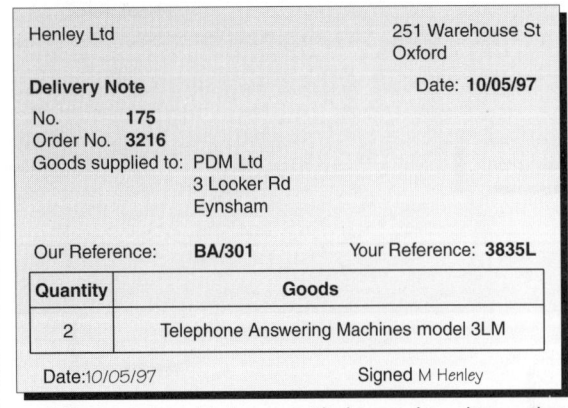

```
Henley Ltd                         251 Warehouse St
                                   Oxford
Delivery Note                      Date: 10/05/97
No.      175
Order No. 3216
Goods supplied to:  PDM Ltd
                    3 Looker Rd
                    Eynsham

Our Reference:  BA/301    Your Reference: 3835L
```

Quantity	Goods
2	Telephone Answering Machines model 3LM

Date:10/05/97   Signed M Henley

- **delivery note** – this is sent with the goods and is used as proof by the sender that the goods arrived.

- **debit and credit notes** – these are used if there is a mistake or refund. A 'debit note' adds to invoices e.g. if the invoice is for £30 instead of £300 a debit note is given for £270. A 'credit note' is used to deduct amounts from the invoice. If the invoice was for £400 not £40 a credit note will be sent for £360. A credit note is also given if goods are faulty.
- **invoice** – this is the bill for the goods and services supplied. It usually has details of the buyer and seller, the order number, details of the goods and services supplied, the amount owed and payment terms (e.g. discounts for early payment). Invoices usually have the abbreviation "E & O E". This means Errors and Omissions Excepted; this protects the supplier if there are any mistakes on the invoice.
- **pro forma invoice** – this type of invoice must be paid BEFORE the goods are delivered.

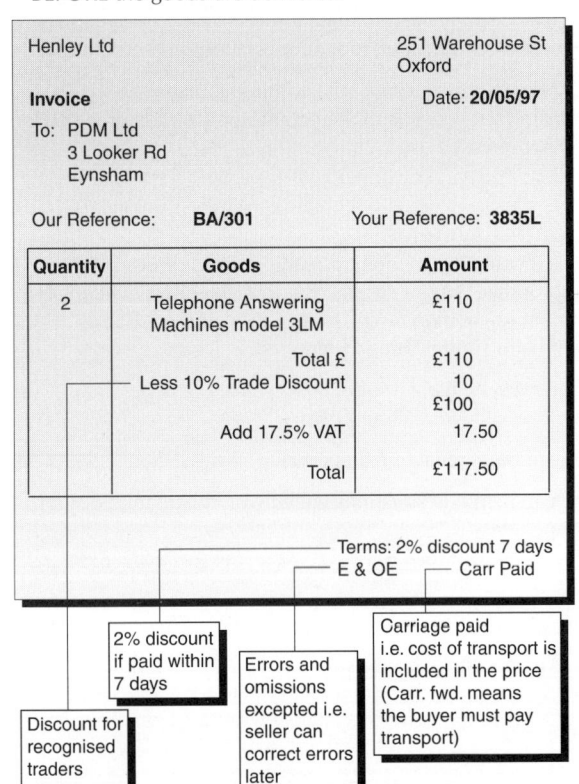

```
Henley Ltd                         251 Warehouse St
                                   Oxford
Invoice                            Date: 20/05/97
To:  PDM Ltd
     3 Looker Rd
     Eynsham

Our Reference:  BA/301    Your Reference: 3835L
```

Quantity	Goods	Amount
2	Telephone Answering Machines model 3LM	£110
	Total £	£110
	Less 10% Trade Discount	10
		£100
	Add 17.5% VAT	17.50
	Total	£117.50

Terms: 2% discount 7 days
E & OE   Carr Paid

- 2% discount if paid within 7 days — Discount for recognised traders
- Errors and omissions excepted i.e. seller can correct errors later
- Carriage paid i.e. cost of transport is included in the price (Carr. fwd. means the buyer must pay transport)

- **statement of account** – this is sent to regular customers showing the amount they have been charged, the amount paid and the outstanding balance

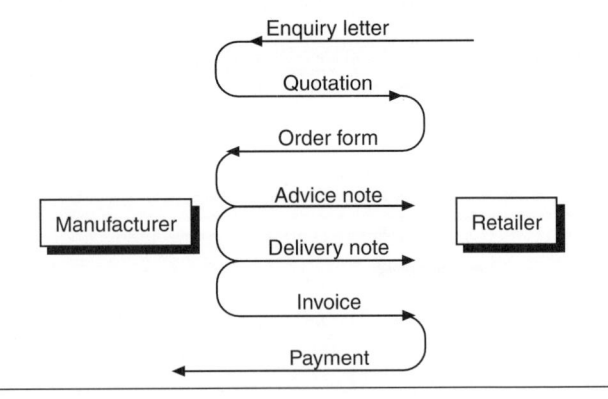

```
             Enquiry letter
             Quotation
             Order form
Manufacturer Advice note      Retailer
             Delivery note
             Invoice
             Payment
```

76 Information and Communication

Success in the 1990s

To be successful in the 1990s firms need to:

Know the market
The key to competitive success lies in knowing what your customers want now and are likely to want in the future. Successful firms are proactive, i.e. they anticipate change rather than react to it.

Know the competition
Firms need to identify their areas of relative strength and weakness; they must monitor the market and measure their levels of cost and service against the competition.

Work with suppliers
The trend in the 1990s is not to select suppliers purely on the basis of price. It is important to consider other factors such as their quality, reliability and delivery schedules. Successful firms involve suppliers and develop a joint problem solving approach; they build long-term relationships with a few trusted suppliers - this is called 'partnership sourcing'.

Design products properly
A good design takes into account internal customers as well as external customers. A well designed product is relatively easy to make as well as satisfying customers' needs and wants.

Get it right and right again and right again
Production processes and the final goods and services must be reliable. Firms continually monitor their performance and develop ways of improving.

Be flexible
Staff and equipment must be flexible to respond quickly to changing needs. This requires training and investment.

Put people together
Managers need to get people to share ideas and learn from each other. By bringing people together they are more likely to understand each others problems and find solutions.

Build a learning organisation
Managers need to encourage people to develop skills and to try out ideas even if they fail at first. People should be encouraged to be curious.

Time competitive
Increasingly firms are competing on time by producing products more quickly and delivering in a shorter time. Products can be developed more quickly by carrying out different parts of the process at the same time rather than waiting for one stage to finish before starting another, i.e. simultaneous engineering rather than a sequential approach. In 1981 Yamaha attacked Honda in the motor bike industry. Honda responded by rapid production development. In 1982 Honda had 60 models of motor bike; over the next 18 months it introduced or replaced 113 models.

Delight the customer
There are so many competitors that firms have to do more than satisfy the customer, they have to delight the customer. (This is Kwik Fit's stated aim). Successful organisations must not only meet customers expectations, they must surpass them. Shopping, for example, must be made a pleasant, interesting and enjoyable experience not a chore. This involves many factors such as: the products which are stocked, the decor of the shop, the aroma in the shop, the image of the store, the way in which customers are served, the way in which people can pay and the after sales service.

The successful organisation in the 1990s will:
- have a clear and shared view of where and how it will be successful (i.e. a mission)
- be able to predict change and respond quickly
- maintain the high levels of quality at an appropriate price
- learn faster than the competition

Test section

This section of the book is intended to help you with your revision. In the first part we look at different types of question that you might encounter, then there is a list of key revision terms, and finally there are revision questions on different areas of the syllabus.

Good luck in your exams!

Types of questions

1 Questions which ask you to state, describe or list

Some questions are designed simply to test your knowledge. If, for example, the question asks you to 'state', 'list' or 'give' factors, you just have to write down the key points. You do not need to develop your ideas.

Example
Question
State two ways in which a firm can raise finance (2)

Answer
- Get a loan
- Sell shares

2 Questions which ask you to explain

If a question asks you to explain, you must develop your point. It is not enough to list ideas - you must show why they are relevant.

Example
Question
State one advantage of a piece rate payment system (1)

Answer
- Leads to higher output

compared to
Question
EXPLAIN one advantage of a piece rate payment system (2)

Answer
- Leads to higher output BECAUSE the more the employee produces the more he or she is paid, and, therefore, he or she has an incentive to make more units.

When you want to explain something, the word 'BECAUSE' is often very useful.

Example
Question
Explain how a cut in income tax can affect firms (4)

Answer
Sales may increase BECAUSE consumers will have more disposable income. Production may have to increase BECAUSE sales are higher (unless the firm already has enough stocks).

3 Questions which refer to a particular firm or situation

Some questions are directly related to the data or case study. For example, 'explain how a cut in income tax can help XYZ Ltd'. To answer questions like these you need to refer to the type of firm and its particular situation.

Imagine, for example, that XYZ produces high quality clothing. Your answer might be:
"A cut in income tax might lead to an increase in sales BECAUSE consumers have more disposable income. With more income, demand for high quality clothing often increases significantly as people treat themselves to a luxury."

If, however, XYZ Ltd produces pencils, your answer might be:
"A cut in income tax might lead to an increase in sales BECAUSE consumers have more disposable income. However, the demand for pencils may not increase very much because pencils are a necessity and so with more money consumers are more likely to buy goods like high quality clothes".

If a particular firm or type of business is mentioned, it is very important to think about what would be appropriate for this type of organisation.

Example
Question
Richard Knowles is a local window-cleaner who has recently set up in business. State two promotional methods which Richard could use to increase the number of his customers. (2)

Answer
- television advertising
- mailshot

The first suggestion is inappropriate for this type of business. It would cost too much and cover too wide an area.
The second idea is better, as it is cheaper and can be targetted on a particular area.

When you are trying to relate your answer to the text, it is often useful to use phrases such as 'in this type of business', 'in this particular case', or 'in this instance'. This will help you to keep relating your answer to the given situation.

4 Questions which have a large number of marks

On some examination boards the questions can appear quite general but have a very large number of marks. For example, 'what are the effects on a firm of a cut in income tax? (8 marks)'

To answer this question successfully, you need to identify a number of effects and develop them in some detail. A very good answer will also comment on the possible effects and show some judgement. For example, the effect of a cut in income tax on a firm not only depends on the type of product, it also depends on:

- the amount the tax has been cut
- whether anything else has changed
  (e.g. other taxes)
- the present situation of the firm
  (e.g. does it have the resources to produce more if demand increases?)

To comment on your answer think about:
- how this firm differs from others
- the resources of the firm
- which of the ideas you have put forward is most important

5 Questions which ask you to advise

If, for example, the question asks you to 'advise XYZ Ltd on the most appropriate means of raising finance', you should discuss the options it has, such as borrowing or selling shares, and then come to a conclusion. For example, "in this case, XYZ has already borrowed quite heavily, interest rates are high and the original owners do not mind bringing in new shareholders, so selling shares would seem a suitable means of raising money."

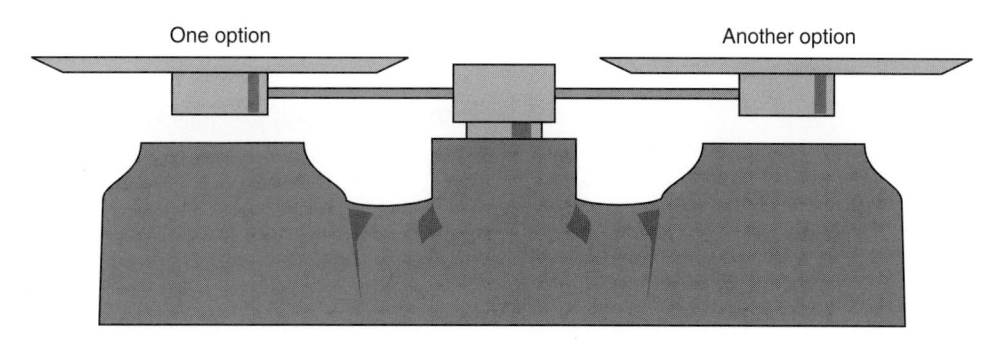

To advise you must examine the various options, weigh them up and decide which is most relevant

Key revision words

Listed below are twenty key revision words for each section of the book. Use these words to test yourself:

Introduction to Business (pages 1-14)

autocratic leadership
business plan
co-operative
directors
external economies of scale
franchise
internal economies of scale
limited liability
mergers
mission statement
monopoly
ordinary shares
partnerships
primary sector
private limited company
public limited company
public sector
secondary sector
sole traders
tertiary sector

Marketing (pages 15-26)

advertising
advertising agency
consumer durables
distribution channel
internal data
loss leader
market orientation
market research
market segment
marketing mix
patent
penetration pricing
primary data
producer goods
promotion
sample
secondary data
skimming pricing
trademark
wholesaler

Finance (pages 27-39)

assets employed (or net assets employed)
break-even
budget
capital employed
conservatism
creditors
current assets
debtors
depreciation
fixed assets
fixed costs
gross profit
liabilities
loan
matching principle
net profit
retained profits
return on capital employed
turnover
working capital

Production (pages 40-43)

automation
batch production
computer aided design
computer aided manufacture
division of labour
enterprise zones
flow production
job production
just in time production
mass production
primary production
productivity

purchasing department
quality control
research and development
secondary production
specialisation
stockholding costs
subcontracting
work study

People Management (pages 44-56)

chain of command
contract of employment
delegation
employment law
equal opportunities
gross pay
health and safety legislation
Herzberg
induction training
industrial action
industrial tribunal
job description
job rotation
Maslow
off the job training
on the job training
piece rate
selection process
span of control
trade union

External Factors (pages 57-70)

central government
corporation tax
Data Protection Act
direct taxes
European Union
exchange rate
Export Credit Guarantee Department
fiscal policy
free market economy

interest rate
income tax
pressure group
privatisation
quotas
recession
regional policy
Sale of Goods Act
structural unemployment
tariff
value added tax

Information and Communication (pages 71-76)

agenda
credit note
database
e mail
fax
formal communication
informal communication
information technology
internal communication
invoice
letter
memo
minutes of a meeting
networks
one way communication
oral communicaton
reports
spreadsheets
visual communication
word-processor

Test section 81

Test questions

On the following pages are a series of test questions on each area of the book. You could use these as part of your revision programme. Marks are in brackets.

Introduction to Business (pages 1-14)

1 State one advantage of being a sole trader compared to a partnership. **(1)**

2 Explain what is meant by the following terms:
   a horizontal integration **(1)**
   b merger **(1)**
   c takeover **(1)**
   d vertical integration **(1)**
   e public corporation **(1)**

3 Explain what is meant by a multinational. **(2)**

4 Explain what is meant by a co-operative. **(2)**

5 What is meant by the 'secondary' sector? **(2)**

6 Explain what is meant by the term the public sector. **(2)**

7 Give two features of a public limited company. **(2)**

8 Identify three business objectives. **(3)**

9 Explain two internal economies of scale a firm might gain from expansion. **(4)**

10 Give two advantages and two disadvantages of owning a franchise. **(4)**

11 Large firms have advantages over small firms so why do so many small firms still exist? **(5)**

12 Why do people set up in business on their own? **(6)**

13 What problems do people face when they set up in business on their own? **(6)**

14 What is usually included in a business plan? **(6)**

15 What are the advantages of setting up as a partnership compared to a sole trader? **(6)**

16 What are the advantages of a private limited company compared to a partnership? **(8)**

17 What problems do small firms have? **(8)**

18 What are the advantages of growth for a firm? **(8)**

Marketing (pages 15-26)

1 Identify two sales promotion methods which could be used when marketing a new improved version of an existing product. **(2)**

2 Explain the following terms:
   a market share **(2)**
   b brand **(3)**
   c market segmentation **(3)**
   d sales promotion **(2)**
   e wholesaler **(2)**

3 Explain what is meant by the term 'consumer durable' with an example. **(3)**

4 A firm decides to launch a new product. Identify one other department in the business which might be affected by this and explain how it might be affected. **(3)**

5 Explain what is meant by skimming pricing. **(4)**

6 Suggest an appropriate medium for advertising the following:
   a jumble sale at the local church
   b new brand of coffee
   c a summer sale on all items
   d the opening of a new nightclub **(4)**

7 Identify four stages in the product life cycle. **(4)**

8 How might the marketing mix of a product change in the maturity stage of the product life cycle? **(4)**

9 State and explain two methods which a firm which is about to launch a new range of clothing might use to research the market. **(4)**

10 What influences the distribution channel a firm chooses for its products? **(6)**

11 What factors need to be taken into account when planning an advertising campaign? **(8)**

12 Flo Jo Ltd produces clothing aimed at the high income group. Sales have been poor recently and the firm has decided to change its marketing to target lower income groups. What changes might it make to its marketing mix? **(8)**

13 How might a firm set its price for a product? **(8)**

14 What is meant by the marketing mix? **(10)**

Finance (pages 27-39)

1 Which one of the following is a fixed cost?
   a piecework payments to workers
   b raw materials
   c components used in production
   d rent **(1)**

2 What is a mortgage loan? **(1)**

3 Identify two groups who might be interested in a firm's accounts **(2)**

4 What is a budget? **(2)**

5 What is meant by working capital? **(2)**

6 State two accounting principles. **(2)**

7 Explain, with examples where appropriate, each of the following terms:
   a Fixed costs **(3)**
   b Variable costs **(3)**
   c Fixed assets **(3)**
   d Debtors **(2)**
   e Creditors **(2)**
   f Leasing **(2)**

82 Test section

8 The cost of a new machine is £10000. It is expected to be used for four years and then sold for £4000. Using the straight line method, calculate the depreciation per year for this machine. **(4)**

9 Why might a sales forecast be useful to a firm? **(4)**

10 For each of the following indicate whether they are an example of revenue or capital expenditure

	revenue expenditure	capital expenditure
purchase of van		
wages		
rent		
purchase of computers		

(4)

11 The variable costs of making a product are £5. The selling price is £15. The fixed costs are £200. What is the break-even level of output? **(5)**

12 Sales revenue   £40 000
   Gross profit   £10 000
   Net profit   £5 000

   Using the above figures, explain and calculate the
   Gross profit margin **(5)**
   Net profit margin **(5)**

13 **Balance sheet for Melcher Ltd as at 14 November 1997**

   Fixed assets   500
   Current assets   150
   Current liabilities   50
   Net assets employed   600
   Bank loan   200
   Share capital   100
   Retained profit   300
   Capital employed   600

   a Calculate the firm's current ratio for 1997. **(6)**
   b If the company made a net profit of £100 in 1997, calculate its return on capital employed. **(6)**

14 How could a firm reduce its cashflow problems? **(8)**

15 How can an individual raise money to start up in business? **(8)**

Production (pages 40-43)

1 Using examples, explain the following terms:
   a batch production **(4)**
   b just in time production **(4)**
   c economies of scale **(4)**

2 How can the government influence a firm's decision to locate? **(4)**

3 What other factors might influence a firm's decision to locate? **(8)**

4 Why is research and development important for a firm? **(6)**

People Management (pages 44-56)

1 Explain what is meant by the following terms:
   a redundancy **(2)**
   b chain of command **(2)**
   c span of control **(2)**
   d delegation **(2)**
   e gross pay **(2)**

2 State two items in a contract of employment. **(2)**

3 What are the advantages of someone specialising in one job? **(4)**

4 What are the reasons why people join a trade union? **(4)**

5 What are the advantages of a trade union to an employer? **(4)**

6 What are the advantages of delegation? **(4)**

7 What are the advantages of a piece rate payment system? **(6)**

8 What are the advantages of training employees? **(6)**

9 How might a supermarket recruit a new shop assistant? **(8)**

10 What information should be included in a job advertisement? **(8)**

11 How might a firm select a new part time shop assistant? **(8)**

12 How can a manager motivate his or her staff? **(8)**

13 What are the advantages of having a motivated workforce? **(8)**

External Factors (pages 57-70)

1 Explain what is meant by the following terms:
   a recession **(2)**
   b privatisation **(2)**
   c tariff **(2)**
   d exchange rate **(2)**
   e invisible exports **(2)**
   f public sector **(2)**
   e structural unemployment **(2)**

2 Give two arguments for and two arguments against privatising an industry. **(4)**

3 What are the advantages to a business of a single European currency? **(4)**

4 Why do some people resist change? **(4)**

5 How might a cut in income tax help a firm? **(4)**

6 In what ways can a pressure group affect a firm? **(4)**

7 How could an increase in interest rates affect a firm? **(6)**

8 What are the advantages to a firm of the UK being a member of the European Union? **(8)**

9 What problems occur when a firm starts to export its products? **(8)**

10 How can technology help a firm? **(8)**

11 In what ways might changes in society affect a firm? **(8)**

12 How might a firm be affected by a big increase in unemployment? **(8)**

Information and Communication (pages 71-76)

1 What is meant by the term 'invoice'? **(2)**

2 What is meant by the term 'formal communication'? **(2)**

3 What is meant by 'two way' communication? **(2)**

4 Distinguish between a spreadsheet and a word processor. **(3)**

5 Distinguish between a letter and a memo. **(3)**

6 Identify three groups with whom a firm must communicate. **(3)**

7 What problems occur to prevent good communication within a firm? **(4)**

8 What do you think is the most apppropriate means of communication for the following messages? Explain your answers.
   a Customers need to be informed about a change in opening hours for your shop
   b Customers need to be informed about a new product you have produced
   c You need to communicate with the bank manager about a loan
   d You need to inform one of your managers that you will be late for a meeting **(4)**

9 What are the advantages to a firm of using information technology? **(8)**

10 Why is good communication important for a firm? **(8)**

Case Study Style Questions

(Remember that where appropriate you should use examples from the Case Study to support your answers)

Watts Ltd

Linda Harris is the Managing Director of a clothing manufacturer called Watts Ltd, which is based in the West Midlands. The business was originally set up as a partnership by Carol and Jim Watts in the 1970s and became a private limited company in 1985. Carol and Jim decided to stop taking a day to day role in the business in 1997, and appointed Linda because they wanted more time to travel and relax. Although they no longer manage the business, they remain the main shareholders owning more than 60% of the company.

Watts Ltd specializes in producing high quality men's clothing, particularly suits. Their clothes are sold in exclusive retail outlets throughout the world and are aimed mainly at high income earners aged 30 to 45. The clothes are marketed under the brand name of "Brookfield".

In the last few years, the sales of the company have been increasing quite rapidly, partly because of the boom in the economy. Given the increase in sales, Watts Ltd is now considering expanding its production capacity by building another factory. As well as increasing the firm's output, this expansion might also lead to economies of scale and greater profitability.

The growth in sales has also meant that the firm has had to recruit quite large numbers of new employees, so that it can produce enough to meet all of its orders. The need to recruit people has been made more urgent because of the high level of labour turnover, particularly amongst the machinists who produce the finished clothes. Although the company pays quite high wages compared to other firms in the area, it is having difficulty keeping staff once they have been recruited. Up until now the staff at Watts Ltd have not been members of a trade union, but in the last few months many of them have started talking about joining one.

As well as building another factory, Linda Harris is also conscious of the need to improve most of the existing equipment that is being used within the firm. Customers are placing greater emphasis on quality in the 1990s and it is important that the clothes her company produces are well made and do not have any faults. Linda is aware that her direct rivals have significantly improved the quality of their products in recent years and that her company needs to be able to match this. She is also worried about competition from the big retailers who are now moving into the clothing market and producing good quality suits for themselves, and selling them under their own brand name. Linda fears that in the future this trend may take away a large part of Watts Ltd's existing business. To try to prevent this, she believes it is essential that the company continues to improve the quality of its clothes, and this means that her employees will need better equipment. Unfortunately, the amount of investment required is quite high and Linda is not sure if the company will be able to raise the finance needed to build a new factory **and** improve its existing machines. Linda thinks that to do both the cost will be at least £1,500,000.

At the same time, Linda is pleased with the new range of suits that the company is about to launch. After undertaking some market research, her managers identified a gap in the market for well made, casual clothes. As a result, Watts Ltd is about to start producing a range of summer suits which will sell at around £300 in the shops. Linda is also looking at the possibility of diversification into other goods such as briefcases, wallets, shoes, and pens.

In the long term, Linda hopes that the business will become a public limited company. She thinks this will put it in a stronger position to compete internationally and has already advised Carol and Jim Watts that, in her view, this is how the business needs to develop.

Watts Ltd

£000s	1994	1995	1996	1997
Sales	2000	2200	3200	4000
Net profit	400	420	440	460

INSTRUCTION : Draw the above as bar charts

Balance Sheet for Watts Ltd as at 14 November 1997

	£ 000
Fixed assets	4000
Current assets	1100
Current liabilities	500
Net current assets (working capital)	600
Net assets employed	**4600**
Financed by :	
Issued share capital	600
Retained profit	2000
Loans	2000
Capital employed	**4600**

Questions   TOTAL MARKS AVAILABLE : 140 marks

1   Total for this question : 30 marks

Explain the meaning of the following terms giving examples. Your examples can be taken from the Case Study or any other source.

- **a** shareholder (3)
- **b** retail outlet (3)
- **c** fixed assets (3)
- **d** retained profit (3)
- **e** diversification (3)
- **f** boom (3)
- **g** brand name (3)
- **h** market research (3)
- **i** current liabilities (3)
- **j** economies of scale (3)

2   Total for this question: 20 marks

- **a** What problems could a high labour turnover cause Watts Ltd? (8)
- **b** Explain how Watts Ltd could recruit new machinists. (6)
- **c** What benefits might the workers at Watts Ltd gain from being in a trade union? (6)

3   Total for this question: 22 marks

- **a** What are the benefits of turning a partnership into a private limited company? (4)
- **b** If the company decides to go ahead and build a new factory as well as improving the equipment in the existing factory it will need to raise around £1,500,000. How do you think it could raise this money? (8)
- **c** Outline the arguments for and against Watts Ltd becoming a public limited company. (10)

4   Total for this question: 28 marks

- **a** Compare the trends in sales and net profit for Watts Ltd from 1994 to 1997. (5)
- **b** Apart from the boom in the economy, what else might have caused the increase in sales of Watts Ltd's products from 1994 to 1997? (5)
- **c** How could Watts Ltd promote the new range of summer casual suits which it is about to launch? (8)
- **d** Explain the factors that the company should take into account before deciding whether to expand the production capacity of the business. (10)

5   Total for this question: 40 marks

- **a** What might be causing the high levels of labour turnover at Watts Ltd? (4)
- **b** The passage states that customers are more concerned about good quality products in the 1990s than in the past. Why do you think this might be? (6)
- **c** Explain the factors which could influence the price that Watts Ltd sets for its suits. (8)
- **d** What are the benefits of trade unions to the managers of a company? (6)
- **e** Explain the types of market research that Watts Ltd might have undertaken to identify the gap in the market for well made casual clothes. (6)
- **f** Explain the factors which Watts Ltd should take into account before deciding whether to diversify. (10)

INDEX

Entries in **bold** type indicate main topic entries

A

accounting principles 28
Accounting Standards Board 28
accounts 28
accounts package 74
accruals 28
accumulated depreciation 31
acid test ratio 33
actuary 14
advertising 25, 26
advertising agency 26
advertising budget 26
advertising media 26
Advisory Conciliation and Arbitration service (ACAS) 50
agenda 72
agents 22
annual report 72
appraisal 47
appreciation of currency 62
articles of association 6
assessor 14
assets employed 29, 35
associate company 7
assurance 14
auditors' report 6
authorised shares 7
authority 55
autocratic management 3
automatic handling systems 41

B

backward integration 11
balance of payments 64
balance sheet 29, 30
banker's draft 13
banks 13
bar chart 73
bar code 74
bargaining 49
batch production 40
bill of exchange 65
bill of lading 65
brand leader 25
branding 25
brands 25
break even 36, 37
British Overseas Trade Board (BOTB) 65
BS 7750 69
budgets 38
buildings and contents insurance 14
business cards 76

business closure 8
business cycle 62
business documents 76
business plan 4

C

capital employed 29
capital items 32
cash flow forecast 38, 39
CD ROM 74
census 17
central government 57
centralisation 56
certificate of insurance 65
certificate of origin 65
certificate of value 65
chain of command 55
change 70
channels of distribution 22
charge cards 13
cheque accounts 13
collective bargaining 49
command economy 59
Common Agricultural Policy 67
communication 71, 72, 73
- vertical 71
- lateral 71
- formal 71
- informal 71
- verbal 71
- one way 71
- two way 71
- barriers 71
- internal 72
- external 72
- written 72
communications package 74
companies 6
company secretary 6
comparative advantage 64
competition policy 61
competitive advantage 1
competitor based pricing 20
computer aided design (CAD) 41
computer aided manufacture (CAM) 41
computer integrated manufacture (CIM) 41
computer numerical control (CNC) 41
computers 73
Confederation of British Industry (CBI) 50
conglomerate 11
conservatism 28
consignment note 76
consistency 28
consultation 49

consumer durables 21
consumer goods 21
consumer law 61
consumer non durables 21
Consumers' Association 69
contract law 61
contracting out 60
control systems 75
convenience goods 21
co-operative 5
copyright 21
cost of sales 32
costs 32, 36
craft unions 49
credit cards 13
credit note 76
creditor days 34, 35
creditor period 34
current assets 29
current liabilities 29
current ratio 33
curriculum vitae 46
customs declaration 65
customs union 64
cyclical unemployment 63

D

data processing 75
Data Protection Act 61
database 74
debit cards 13
debit note 76
debtor collection period 34
debtor days 34, 35
debtors 29, 30
decentralisation 56
deed of partnership 5
deindustrialisation 63
delayering 55
delegation 52
delivery note 76
demand based pricing 20
demarcation lines 52
democratic management 3
deposit accounts 13
depreciation 31
direct costs 36
direct debit 13
direct mailing 25
direct taxes 58
directors 6
discipline procedure 47
diseconomies of scale 11
dismissal 47
distribution 22, 23
division of labour 40
drawings 30

E

economic environment 62
electronic mail (e mail) 73
electronic point of sale (EPOS) 74
Employers' Association 50
employment 47
employment laws 50, 61
empowerment 52
enquiry letter 76
enterprise zones 42
entrepreneur 4
environmental issues 69
equal opportunities procedure 47
Equal Pay Act 61
ethics 69
Europe 66, 67
European Monetary Union 67
European Union 66, 67
exchange rates 62
exclusive distribution 23
expenses 32
experiment 17
expert systems 74
Export Credits Guarantee Department (ECGD) 65
export document 65
export invoice 65
export licence 65
exporting problems 65
exports 64
extension strategy 20
extensive distribution 23
external data 16
external economies of scale 11
external finance 27
external growth 10

F

Factories Act 61
fair dismissal 47
Fair Trading Act 61
family brands 25
fax 73, 74
fidelity insurance 14
financial accounting 28
financial efficiency ratios 33, 34
fixed assets 29
fixed costs 36
flexible manufacturing system (FMS) 41
flexible working patterns 48
flotation 6
flow production 40
forecasts 38
foreign currency accounts 13
forward integration 11
franchises 8
free market 59
free trade 64
frictional unemployment 63
fringe benefits 53
FTSE 7
functions of the business 12

G

General National Vocational Qualifications (GNVQs) 47
general union 49
geographical mobility 63
government 57
government objectives 58
greenfield site 42
grievance procedure 47
gross pay 54
gross profit 32
gross profit margin 33
growth 10

H

Health and Safety at Work Act 61
health insurance 14
Herzberg 51
historic cost 31
holding company 7
horizontal integration 11

I

idle time 40
imports 64
incentive schemes 53
income tax 54
indirect costs 36
indirect tax 58
industrial action 49
industrial inertia 42
industrial relations 49
industrial tribunal 47
industry unions 49
information technology 74, 75
informative advertising 26
inputs 1
insolvency 8
Institute of Directors 69
insurance 14
insurance broker 14
insurance cover 14
insurance underwriter 14
integration 11
interest rates 62
internal data 17
internal economies of scale 11
internal finance 27
international competitiveness 64
International Monetary Fund (IMF) 65
international trade 64, 65
internet 73
interviewing 46
invisible items 64
invoice 76
issued shares 7

J

jargon 71
job advertisement 45
job analysis 45

job description 45
job enlargement 52
job enrichment 52
job evaluation 45
job production 40
job rotation 52
job satisfaction 51
joint ventures 8
just in time production 41

K

key man cover 14

L

labour turnover 44
laissez faire management 3
legal environment 61
letter of credit 65
letterheads 76
levels of distribution 22
liabilities 29
line chart (graph) 73
line relationship 56
liquidity ratios 33
Lloyds of London 14
loan guarantee scheme 9
loans 27
local area network (LANs) 75
local government 57
location 42
logo 21
long term finance 27
long term liabilities 29
loss leader 20

M

management 3
management accounting 28
management buy outs 8
management hierarchy 3
management information systems 74
management skills 3
management style 3
margin of safety 36
mark up pricing 20
market capitalisation 6
market orientation 15
market segmentation 18
market share 15
market size 15
marketing 15
marketing mix 15
marketing research 16
Maslow 51
mass market 15
mass production 40
master budget 38
materiality 28
medium term finance 27
memo 72
memorandum of association 6

merchandising 25
merger 10
mission statement 3
mixed economy 59
money 13
money market accounts 13
Monopolies and Mergers
    Commission 61
monopoly 12
motivation in practice 52
motivation in theory 51
multi-skilling 52

N

national income 62
national insurance 54
National Vocational Qualifications
    (NVQs) 47
nationalised industries 5
needs 51, 52
net assets 29, 30
net book value 31
net current assets 30
net pay 54
net profit 32
net profit margin 33
networks 75
newsletter 72
niche market 15
non profit organisations 5
noticeboards 72

O

objectives 2
observation 17
occupational mobility 63
off line systems 75
off the job training 47
offer for sale 7
office automation 74
oligopoly 12
on line systems 75
on the job training 47
operating system 74
order form 76
ordinary shares 7
organic growth 10
organisational chart 55
organisations 1
outputs 1
overheads 36
own label brands 25

P

partnership 5
patent 21
paternalistic management 3
pay slip 54
payment systems 53
penetration pricing 20
pension 54

people 44
performance related pay 53
person specification 45
personal selling 25
personnel 44
personnel (or people) planning 44
persuasive advertising 26
pie chart 73
piece rate 53
placing 7
population 17
predatory pricing 20
preference shares 7
pressure groups 69
price 20
price discrimination 20
primary production 40
primary research 16
primary sector 1
private company 6
private sector 59
privatisation 60
pro forma invoice 76
producer co-operative 5
producer goods 21
product 21
product differentiation 21
product life cycle 19
product orientation 15
production 40
production budget 38
production department 40
productivity 40
profit and loss statement 32
profit v cash 32
profitability ratios 33
progressive tax 58
promotion 25
promotional mix 25
protectionism 64
prudence principle 28
psychological pricing 20
public issue 7
public limited company 6
public relations 25
public sector 5, 59
purchasing 43

Q

qualitative research 16
quality control 40
quotation 76

R

Race Relations Act 61
ratios 33
real time 75
realisation principle 28
recession 62
recruitment and selection 45, 46
reducing balance depreciation 31
redundancy 48
Redundancy Payments Act 61

regional assistance 42
regional enterprise grants 42
regional policy 57
regressive tax 58
reports 34
research and development 40
reserves 29, 30
residual value 31
resignation 47
resistance to change 70
responsibility 55
retail co-operative 5
retailers 24
retirement 47
revenue items 32
reward systems 53
rights issue 7
robots 41

S

salary 53
Sale of Goods Act 61
sales budget 38
sales forecast 38
sales promotion 25
samples 17
savings 13
seasonal unemployment 63
secondary production 40
secondary research 16
secondary sector 1
segmentation 18
selective distribution 23
selective regional assistance 42
semi variable costs 36
Sex Discrimination Act 61
share capital 7
share price 7
shares 7, 27
shopping goods 21
short term finance 27
Single European Act 66
size of firms 10
skimming pricing 20
small firms 9
social audit 69
social trends 68
socio-economic groups 18
software 74
sole trader 5
sources of finance 27
span of control 55
specialisation 40
specific tax 58
sponsorship 25
spreadsheets 74
staff relationship 56
stages of the product life cycle 19
stakeholders 12
standing order 13
statement of account 76
stock control 43
stock exchange 7
stock turnover 34, 35

stockholding costs 43
stocks 43
straight line depreciation 31
structural unemployment 63
subcontracting 40
subsidiary 7
survey 17

T

take-over 10
tax codes 54
taxation 58
technology 41
tertiary production 40
tertiary sector 1
time rate 53
total assets 29, 31
total revenue 36
trade cycle 62
Trade Descriptions Act 61
Trade Union Congress (TUC) 50
trade war 64
trademark 21
training 47
Training and Enterprise Councils 47
transport 24

U

underwriter 14
unemployment 63
unfair dismissal 47
union recognition 49
union strength 49
unions 49, 50
unique selling proposition (USP) 1
United Nations Conference on Trade
  and Development (UNCTAD) 65

V

value added tax 57
variable costs 36
vertical integration 11
video conferencing 73, 74
visible items 64
visual communication 73

W

Weights and Measures Act 61
white collar unions 49
wholesaler co-operative 5
wholesalers 22
wide area networks (WANs) 75
word processor 74
work study 40
working capital 29, 30
working capital ratio 33, 35
World Trade Organisation 64